NATIONS OF THE WORLD

INDONESIA

Edward Horton

www.raintreepublishers.co.uk

Visit our website to find out more information about **Raintree** books.

To order:

 Phone 44 (0) 1865 888113

 Send a fax to 44 (0) 1865 314091

 Visit the Raintree bookshop at www.raintreepublishers.co.uk to browse our catalogue and order online.

First published in Great Britain by Raintree, Halley Court, Jordan Hill, Oxford, OX2 8EJ, part of Harcourt Education Ltd.
Raintree is a registered trademark of Harcourt Education Ltd.

Produced for Raintree by the Brown Reference Group plc
Project Editor: Dawn Titmus
Designer: Graham Curd
Picture Researcher: Susy Forbes
Cartographers: Mark Walker and Peter Bull
Editorial Assistant: Tom Webber
Indexer: Kay Ollerenshaw
Consultant: Clive Carpenter

Raintree Publishers
Editor: Kate Buckingham

Printed and bound in Singapore.

ISBN 1 844 43243 2
08 07 06 05 04
10 9 8 7 6 5 4 3 2 1

British Library cataloguing in publication data
Horton, Edward
Indonesia
915.9'8
A full catalogue is available for this book from the British Library.

Acknowledgements
Front cover: Balinese dancer
Title page: Buddha statue at Borobudur, Java

The acknowledgements on page 128 form part of this copyright page.

Every effort has been made to contact copyright holders of any material reproduced in this book. Any omissions will be rectified in subsequent printings if notice is given to the publishers.

Contents

Foreword 5

Introduction.................................7

Land and cities....................13

Past and present.................49

The economy 83

Arts and living 99

The future...........................117

Almanac...............................120

Timeline..............................122

Glossary..............................124

Bibliography 125

Index....................................126

Foreword

Since ancient times, people have gathered together in communities where they could share and trade resources and strive to build a safe and happy environment. Gradually, as populations grew and societies became more complex, communities expanded to become nations – groups of people who felt sufficiently bound by a common heritage to work together for a shared future.

Land has usually played an important role in defining a nation. People have a natural affection for the landscape in which they grew up. They are proud of its natural beauties – the mountains, rivers and forests – and of the towns and cities that flourish there. People are proud, too, of their nation's history – the shared struggles and achievements that have shaped the way they live today.

Religion, culture, race and lifestyle, too, have sometimes played a role in fostering a nation's identity. Often, though, a nation includes people of different races, beliefs and customs. Many may have come from distant countries. Nations have rarely been fixed, unchanging things, either territorially or racially. Throughout history, borders have changed, often under the pressure of war, and people have migrated across the globe in search of a new life or because they are fleeing from oppression or disaster. The world's nations are still changing today – some nations are breaking up and new nations are forming.

Indonesia is an island nation located in Southeast Asia. It is a relatively new country, having gained its independence from the Netherlands in 1949. Historically, it stood at the crossroads of the great trading routes between Asia and Europe. Traders from all over the world went to the Indonesian islands in search of the spices that they hoped would make them rich. Today, it is the biggest Muslim nation in the world, and is also home to a diverse range of cultures and races. It is a land of stunningly beautiful landscapes and magnificent ancient monuments, but it is also a place where conflict and violence between religious groups occur only too frequently.

Introduction

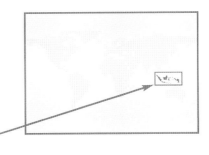

The archipelago (group of islands) of Indonesia has an astonishing variety of people, wildlife and landscapes contained within its borders. It is home to some 200 **ethnic groups** who speak more than 400 languages and **dialects**. Indonesia is also a land of stark contrasts. One of the cradles of the human race, it is one of the most recently created major nations. It has the largest **Muslim** population of any country in the world, yet its oldest cultural monuments are Buddhist and Hindu. It is the third most populous **democracy** in the world (after India and the United States), but is not fully democratic and suffers frequent unrest. Indonesia possesses huge valuable natural resources, yet it remains plagued by poverty and inequality.

For visitors, Indonesia offers a unique blend of natural marvels and cultural diversity – as well as endless kilometres of beaches, many of them empty. Great national parks invite walkers to roam through some of the world's outstanding wild places, where the very rarest rhinos and tigers are making their last stand against the threat of extinction. The fabulous temples and palaces preserved from earlier times provide fascinating insights into Indonesia's past. Ancient traditions live on in the enchanting music of the **gamelan** orchestra and the all-night storytelling of the Javanese shadow-puppet theatre.

As the sun rises in Java, Muslim worshippers mark the end of Ramadan.
Indonesia is the nation with the world's largest Muslim population.

FACT FILE

● Jakarta, the capital of Indonesia, is a sprawling, congested city of more than 11 million people. Gleaming new skyscrapers stand next to slums and shanty towns.

● With nearly 150 million people, Java is one of the most heavily populated islands in the world. It covers only 6.9% of Indonesia's land area yet has 60% of the population.

● Indonesia is the largest Muslim-majority country.

● The islands of Indonesia stretch more than 5000 km (3000 miles) from the Asian mainland, in the west, to the Pacific Ocean, in the east.

The 10,000 rupiah note features the portrait of Sultan Hamengku, governor of Yogyakarta.

NAME AND MONEY

Before Indonesia officially became independent from the Netherlands in 1949, it was known as the Dutch East Indies. Today, its official name is the Republic of Indonesia (or Republik Indonesia in the official language, Bahasa Indonesia).

Indonesia's currency is the rupiah (Rp for short). Since 1997, the rupiah has plummeted in value, hitting its lowest point in January 1998. Since then, the currency has stabilized but has never regained its former value. There are notes of 100, 500, 1000, 5000, 10,000, 20,000 and 50,000 rupiah, and coins are minted in 25, 50, 100 and 500 rupiah.

The flag

The Indonesian flag is made up of two equal bands of colour – red on top, white at the bottom – and its width is two-thirds its length. The flag was hoisted in Jakarta on 17 August 1945, when Indonesia declared its independence from the Netherlands. At the time, Indonesia was occupied by the Japanese.

POPULATION

The population of Indonesia is officially estimated at around 207 million, which makes it the fourth most populated country in the world, after China, India and the United States. Most Indonesian people are of Austronesian origin (from the central and south Pacific), along with ethnic Chinese, Indians, and Arabs. The major ethnic groups by percentage are Javanese (41.7), Sundanese (15.4), Malays (3.5), Madurese (3.3), Batak (3.0), Minangkabau (2.7) and Betawi (2.5).

The national anthem

The Indonesian national anthem is called 'Indonesia Raya', which means 'Great Indonesia'. It was written by Wage Rudolf Supratman and introduced at the All Indonesian Youth Congress in 1928. With their strong plea for national unity, the lyrics were recognized by Indonesians as a spirited attack on the Dutch colonial policy of divide and rule. This policy tried to reinforce differences of religion, language and culture between the many Indonesian peoples. The patriotic song caught on quickly with those young people who wanted Indonesia's independence. The song served as an unofficial anthem until the proclamation of a republic in 1945, when it received official status.

Indonesia, my native land,
My place of birth,
Where I stand guard
Over my motherland.

Indonesia, my nationality,
My people and my country,
Let us all cry
For united Indonesia.

Long live my land,
Long live my country,
My nation and all my people.

Arouse their spirit,
Arouse their bodies,
For Great Indonesia.

Great Indonesia,
Free and independent,
The land, the country I love.

Great Indonesia,
Free and independent,
Long live Indonesia.

More than two-thirds of the population live on the relatively small islands of Java and Bali. Java is where the capital, Jakarta, is located and is the centre of political, economic and cultural power. In contrast, the larger outlying islands, especially in eastern Indonesia, are sparsely populated. Papua (the western half of the island of New Guinea) comprises 22 per cent of Indonesia's land mass, yet is home to only 1 per cent of its population. Similarly, Kalimantan, on the island of Borneo, makes up 28 per cent of Indonesia's land area and is home to only 5 per cent of the population.

POPULATION DENSITY

The population of Indonesia is very unevenly distributed and is concentrated on the islands of Java and Bali. Java is just over half the area of the UK, yet it is home to almost 150 million people – a density of nearly 1000 people per square kilometre (2590 per square mile). By contrast, Kalimantan and Papua are very thinly populated.

PERSONS

Per sq km	Per sq mile
30	80
50	130
100	260
500	1300

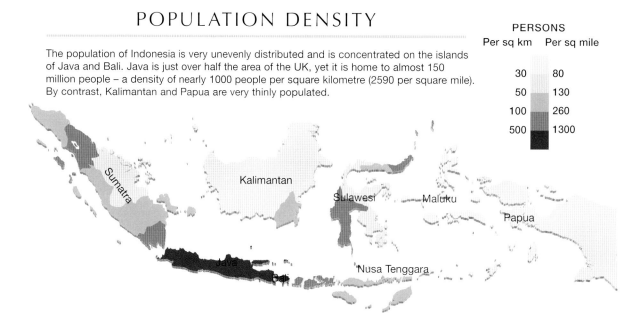

Indonesia's population is growing at the rate of about 1.5 per cent per year. By 2035, it is estimated to reach 330 million.

INDONESIA'S POPULATION

millions

source: Library of Congress/Federal Research Division

LANGUAGE AND RELIGION

There are hundreds of languages and dialects in Indonesia. The official language is Bahasa Indonesia, which is based on the Malay language. Bahasa Indonesia is the most widely spoken language, even though it is most people's second language. Without a common language, Indonesians would find it difficult to communicate with each other. Within family and ethnic groups, people speak in their native tongue. They use Bahasa Indonesia for communicating outside the group. The most widely spoken first language is Javanese. In the capital, Jakarta, people who work in international business usually speak English. Some older Indonesians speak Dutch – a reminder of days before independence from the Netherlands.

Although Indonesia is a secular state – that is, religion is kept separate from politics – the state is based on

WHERE DOES INDONESIA'S POPULATION LIVE?

43%
cities and towns

57%
countryside

the five philosophical principles of Pancasila (pronounced *pan-cha-see-la*), which means 'five principles'. The first principle is that all citizens believe in one God (this can mean any god, not just the Muslim Allah). The other four principles are: a just and civilized humanity; the unity of Indonesia; guided democracy (see page 74) arising from representative government; and peace and social justice.

About 88 per cent of Indonesians claim to be Muslims, and there are more Muslims than there are members of any other religious group. However, Muslims, like Indonesians who belong to other religions, find different ways to mix their roles as citizens in the country of Indonesia with their adherence to a world religion and with the customs of their local ethnic group.

Nine per cent of the population are Christians, many of whom live in Kalimantan, Sulawesi, Maluku and Papua. The small remaining percentage of Indonesians are mostly Hindu or Buddhist. While these ancient Indian religions have few members in Indonesia, they have a profound influence on Indonesian culture, which is apparent in everything from temple architecture to music and dance.

Like many countries in Asia, Indonesia has a young population – almost 60 per cent are under the age of 30.

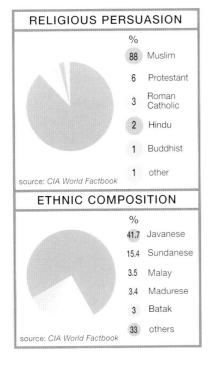

RELIGIOUS PERSUASION

%	
88	Muslim
6	Protestant
3	Roman Catholic
2	Hindu
1	Buddhist
1	other

source: *CIA World Factbook*

ETHNIC COMPOSITION

%	
41.7	Javanese
15.4	Sundanese
3.5	Malay
3.4	Madurese
3	Batak
33	others

source: *CIA World Factbook*

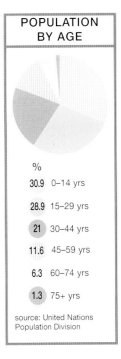

POPULATION BY AGE

%	
30.9	0–14 yrs
28.9	15–29 yrs
21	30–44 yrs
11.6	45–59 yrs
6.3	60–74 yrs
1.3	75+ yrs

source: United Nations Population Division

Land and cities

'Bhinneka Tunggal Ika – Unity in diversity.'

Indonesia's national motto

Indonesia is the largest archipelago in the world. The chain of about 17,500 islands stretches for more than 5000 kilometres (3000 miles) and straddles the equator between the Indian and Pacific oceans. Indonesia's land area is 1.9 million square kilometres (734,000 square miles), which is almost three and a half times the size of France. There are vast stretches of ocean between many of the islands, of which about 6000 are named and inhabited. Of the inhabited islands, it is thought that no more than 1000 have permanent settlements.

Although the whole of Indonesia lies within the tropics, its geography is extremely varied. There are glaciers in the towering central highlands of Papua and vast tropical swamps in eastern Sumatra. Most of the islands are volcanic (see map on page 17). There are more than 300 volcanoes, of which around 75 are active, and two of which have been responsible for the most violent eruptions in history. The volcanoes run in an arc from Sumatra through Java, Bali and the islands of Nusa Tenggara province north to Maluku and Sulawesi. The reason for this so-called Ring of Fire is that two of the plates that make up the Earth's crust are moving past each other, allowing **magma** from deep within the Earth to reach the surface. Because of its location on the Ring of Fire, Indonesia is vulnerable to earthquakes as well as to volcanic eruptions.

Although Java is one of the most densely populated islands in the world, many areas of natural beauty remain, such as this landscape in central Java.

FACT FILE

- Indonesia has more active volcanoes than any other country and there are several major eruptions every year.

- The mountains of Papua straddle the equator, yet the highest of them are glacial and snow-capped.

- Indonesia is home to a unique mixture of Oriental and Australasian wildlife and plants.

- Recent evidence from satellite images reveals that there may be 18,108 islands in the Indonesian archipelago. However, the Indonesian Hydro-Oceanographic office puts the figure at 17,508.

Indonesia is home to many of the world's most important wilderness areas and wildlife reserves.

Being a volcano hotspot has brought some benefits to Indonesia. Volcanic ash is rich in chemical nutrients, and Indonesia has some of the world's most fertile soil.

PROVINCES AND REGIONS

Indonesia is divided into 28 provinces and three special areas (see map on page 22). However, it is usual when describing the country to group those provinces together into eight distinct regions. These are Java, Sumatra, Bali, Nusa Tenggara, Kalimantan, Sulawesi, Maluku and Papua. In general, the islands' coastal fringe is where trade, commerce, maritime life and exposure to ideas from outside take place, while the interiors are more mountainous and self-contained.

The island of Java

Home to nearly 60 per cent of the country's population, Java is the political, economic and cultural heart of the nation. This long, narrow island stretches for 1060 kilometres (660 miles) from west to east. At its widest, it is 200 kilometres (125 miles) across. A central spine of volcanic mountains extends the length of the island.

Pulau Dua bird sanctuary

Pulau Dua is a small, low-lying island about 1 kilometre (1/2 mile) from the port of Banten on the north-west coast of Java. At low tide, visitors can reach it by foot across mud flats from Banten. At other times, they go by boat. Since 1937, it has been a protected area for migratory birds, about 15,000 of which visit during the breeding season from March to July. Despite its small area of only 8 hectares (20 acres), Pulau Dua is prized as one of Asia's finest bird sanctuaries. Visitors can watch the various bird colonies, resident and migrant, from observation towers located close to nesting sites. Birds that can be seen include egrets, pelicans, herons, cormorants and sea eagles, as well as parrots and parakeets.

~INDONESIA~

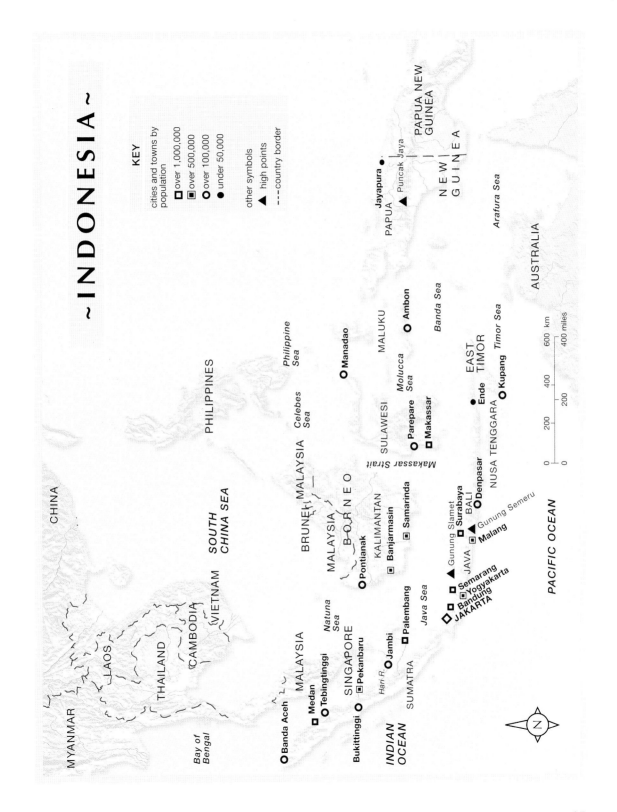

KEY

cities and towns by population

▢ over 1,000,000
▣ over 500,000
○ over 100,000
● under 50,000

other symbols

▲ high points
--- country border

MYANMAR

CHINA

LAOS

THAILAND

VIETNAM

CAMBODIA

PHILIPPINES

Philippine
Sea

SOUTH
CHINA SEA

Bay of
Bengal

○ Banda Aceh

MALAYSIA

Natuna
Sea

▢ Medan
○ Tebingtinggi

SINGAPORE ○
▣ Pekanbaru

Bukittinggi ○

Hari R.

○ Jambi

MALAYSIA

BRUNEI

BORNEO

○ Pontianak

KALIMANTAN

▣ Banjarmasin

▣ Samarinda

Celebes
Sea

○ Manadao

SULAWESI

MALUKU

○ Ambon

Molucca
Sea

○ Parepare
▣ Makassar

Banda Sea

Makassar Strait

SUMATRA

▣ Palembang

Java Sea

▢ JAKARTA
▣ Bandung
▣ Yogyakarta
▲ Semarang
Gunung Slamet ▲ JAVA
▣ Surabaya
Gunung Semeru
▲ Malang
BALI
○ Denpasar

NUSA TENGGARA

EAST
TIMOR
● Ende
○ Kupang

Timor Sea

PACIFIC OCEAN

INDIAN
OCEAN

PAPUA NEW
GUINEA

Puncak Jaya
Jayapura ●
▲
PAPUA

NEW
GUINEA

Arafura Sea

AUSTRALIA

N

0   200   400   600 km
0   200   400 miles

These fall to a flat coastal plain and the brackish waters of the Java Sea, in the north, and the crashing waves of the Indian Ocean on the rugged southern shoreline.

Java is an island of immense natural beauty, from the tropical lowland rainforest of Ujung Kulon National Park, on the south-western tip of the island, to the magnificent volcanic scenery of east Java. It is one of the most densely populated islands in the world, able to sustain a large rural population because of the fertility of its soil, especially in central Java. However, despite its natural beauty and fertile soil, the island is facing severe ecological problems. People are cutting down trees for firewood at an alarming rate, causing the forests to disappear, while pollution levels are great cause for concern, especially in and around Indonesia's two largest cities, Jakarta and Surabaya.

The island of Sumatra

This huge island straddles the equator and is about 1750 kilometres (1100 miles) long and 370 kilometres (230 miles) across at its widest point. In comparison with Java, Sumatra is rugged and wild, with some of the most dramatic landscapes in the world.

Like Java, it has a spine of volcanic mountains, which runs down the western edge of the island. This volcanic backbone is called Bukit Barisan, which means 'Parade of Mountains'. Of the 93 peaks, the highest is Mount Kerinci at 3805 metres (12,483 feet). Some fifteen of the volcanoes are still active. In northern Sumatra, Lake Toba, which was formed by a volcanic eruption thousands of years ago (see box on page 23), provides strong evidence of the explosive power of volcanoes. In the north – the provinces of Aceh and North Sumatra – the mountains rise steeply from the Indian Ocean. Further south, there is a narrow strip of lowland running along the coast.

There are many fine, white sandy beaches on the west coast and on the chain of reef-enclosed islands off the coast. The rugged central highlands of north-west and

The island groups off the west coast of Sumatra, such as Nias Island, are older than the rest of Sumatra in geological terms.

INDONESIA'S VOLCANOES

▲ active volcano

south-west Sumatra remain remote and wild places. Gunung Leuser National Park (see box on pages 24–5) in North Sumatra provides visitors with a rare opportunity to explore one of the world's great unspoiled wildernesses. It is home to four of the world's rarest animals – tigers, rhinoceros, elephants and orangutans.

The contrast between the east and west sides of Sumatra is very marked. Almost the entire eastern side is continuous lowland and saltwater swamp, as enormous river systems meander across the plain to the Strait of Malacca and the South China Sea. The extensive **mangrove** forests of eastern Sumatra are home to many plant and animal species.

A central spine of volcanic mountains runs in an arc through Indonesia. The country lies along the Pacific Ring of Fire – the area where two of the Earth's plates are pushing against each other. Magma from within the Earth comes to the surface, causing volcanoes to form.

The island of Bali

Bali has long been the main focus of Indonesia's tourist industry and enjoys worldwide fame as a tropical island paradise. As though to reflect such a heavenly reputation, the Balinese have traditionally believed that their island belonged to the gods. The natural beauty of Bali is certainly remarkable.

Bali is separated from the eastern tip of Java by the narrow, relatively shallow Bali Strait. During the last Ice Age, there was a land bridge connecting the two. Bali is

Krakatau

About 40 kilometres (25 miles) off the west Java coast lie remnants of the island of Krakatau, also widely known as Krakatoa. In the 17th century, the Dutch East India Company used the island as a source of timber, but it was never settled. Dominated by three volcanic cones, which jutted some 865 m (2667 ft) above sea level, the island announced its presence to the world in the most dramatic manner in 1883.

After months of activity, on the afternoon of 26 August, Krakatau was rocked by a series of massive eruptions. The eruptions continued without pause until the following morning, draining the volcano chamber of its molten magma and rock and undermining the structural support of the cones. Just after 10 a.m., the three cones collapsed into the chasm beneath. Sea water poured into the boiling crater, which caused one final spectacular eruption. The island of Krakatau blew apart in the largest explosion in recorded history. It has been estimated that the force of the explosion was 2000 times that of the atomic bomb that destroyed the Japanese city of

The immense eruption of Krakatau left only one-third of the original island above sea level. Anak Krakatau (Child of Krakatau) appeared in 1928 at about the same spot where the eruption began and has been growing ever since.

This lithograph shows Krakatau in May 1883, three months before its massive eruption. The print was based on a photograph taken by geologists working for Britain's Royal Society.

Hiroshima in 1945. The cost in human life and physical destruction was immense.

Rock and dust were hurled at least 16 kilometres (10 miles) away and possibly twice that distance into the sky. Carried by winds, debris from the explosion fell on the island of Madagascar thousands of kilometres away across the Indian Ocean. The explosion was heard in Sri Lanka off the south-east coast of India and on both sides of the Australian continent. For the following three years, dust and ash particles from Krakatau circled the globe, creating spectacular sunsets all over the world.

However, the explosion and its fall-out were not directly responsible for the enormous loss of life. Huge ocean waves called tsunamis radiated outwards from the epicentre of the explosion at speeds estimated at 480 km/h (300 mph), reaching heights of 30 m (100 ft).

These terrifying waves wiped out about 300 villages in west Java and southern Sumatra, killing over 36,000 people. Slowed down initially by the islands, the tsunamis gathered even more speed once they reached the open sea, racing around the world. The surge was felt in the English Channel, and boats moored on the Alaskan coast started rocking. What had been a highly conspicuous volcanic island was now a 300 m (1000 ft) marine trench.

Ujung Kulon National Park

At the far south-western tip of Java lies a forested peninsula and a few offshore islands that, together with the waters around them, make up Ujung Kulon National Park. The triangular peninsula is connected to mainland Java by a narrow stretch of land and is a completely untamed wilderness. Few people visit it, yet it is one of the great natural delights of Indonesia.

It was first given protected status by Indonesia's Dutch rulers in 1921 and is now listed as a World Heritage site. In all, the park covers about 1200 sq kilometres (470 sq miles). Much of it comprises tropical lowland rainforest, while the surrounding waters sustain coral reefs and an abundant marine life.

The park is home to some 30 species of mammals, including leopards, wild buffalo and several monkeys, such as the extremely endangered Javan gibbon. Bird life is abundant, as are snakes and monitor lizards.

Ujung Kulon's main claim to fame, however, and the reason it was established, is as a haven for the single-horned Javan rhinoceros. It has long been on the verge of extinction, killed by poachers for its horn, which is valued in traditional Chinese medicine. There are only two small groups of these animals in the wild (the other was recently discovered in Vietnam), and it is one of the very rarest of all mammals. The park's population numbers only about 60 individuals, so visitors are unlikely to spot one. The Javan rhinoceros is smaller than its African relative and tends to seek the cover of thick forest.

much smaller than its neighbour, measuring 140 kilometres (87 miles) by 80 kilometres (50 miles). At Bali's core are six volcanic peaks, an extension of Java's central range. The highest of the six, Gunung Agung, rises to just over 3142 metres (10,308 feet) and is traditionally believed to be the home of the gods.

As elsewhere in Indonesia, the volcanoes have determined the island's landscape. The peaks catch the rain clouds that drift in from the Indian Ocean and ensure plentiful rainfall. The many rivers and streams that flow south from their mountain sources provide rich nutrients for the slopes and lowlands. Over many hundreds of years, the Balinese have constructed elaborate irrigation systems that have made the island very fertile.

Madura Island

The city of Surabaya in Java attracts few tourists, so the nearby island of Madura, just half an hour away by ferry, remains one of Indonesia's undiscovered gems. It is lozenge-shaped, measuring 160 kilometres (100 miles) by 30–35 kilometres (19–22 miles). The island terrain is mainly undulating, treeless and infertile, but is suitable for growing tobacco and raising cattle.

While it is part of the province of East Java, its 3 million inhabitants are proudly Madurese, not Javanese, maintaining their own language and culture even when they move to mainland Java.

Apart from a wealth of beautiful, empty white beaches, Madura has one outstanding tourist draw. From August to October, bull-racing becomes a consuming passion for the Madurese.

Called Kerapan Sapi, the bull races have developed from simple ploughing competitions in distant times into today's thrilling spectacle. They progress from local and regional competitions to the all-Madura championship, which is held in the island's capital, Pamekasan.

In the run-up to the final, the Kerapan Besar, Pamekasan's normally quiet streets come alive with costumed parades, dancing and gamelan orchestras. The bulls are pampered with a daily diet of herbs and honey and dozens of eggs – massages also help get them into tip-top condition. They race in yoked pairs over a distance of 120 m (390 ft). They cover the distance in a frenzied ten seconds or so, with the jockey perched on a pair of skids between them (see below). More colourful parades mark the finale.

PROVINCES OF INDONESIA

There are 27 provinces in Indonesia, three special regions – Aceh, Yogyakarta and Papua – and one special capital district – Jakarta. The map shows all the provinces and provincial capitals (marked •), together with a list of their names, apart from Jakarta, which is too small to be shown.

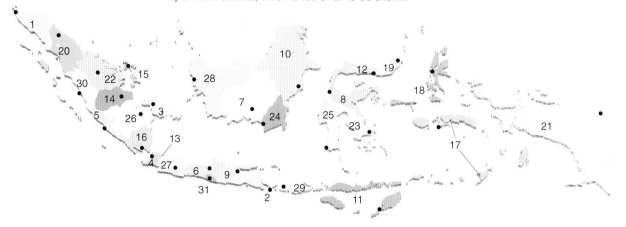

1. ACEH Banda Aceh
2. BALI Denpasar
3. BANGKA-BELITUNG Pangkalpinang
4. BANTEN Serang
5. BENGKULU Bengkulu
6. CENTRAL JAVA Semarang
7. CENTRAL KALIMANTAN
   Palangkaraya
8. CENTRAL SULAWESI Palu
9. EAST JAVA Surabaya
10. EAST KALIMANTAN Samarinda

11. EAST NUSA TENGGARA Kupang
12. GORONTALO Gorontalo
13. JAKARTA Jakarta
14. JAMBI Jambi (Telanaipura)
15. KEPULAUAN RIAU Tanjungpinang
16. LAMPUNG Bandar Lampung
17. MALUKU Ambon
18. NORTH MALUKU Sofifi
19. NORTH SULAWESI Manado
20. NORTH SUMATRA Medan
21. PAPUA Jayapura

22. RIAU Pakanbaru
23. SOUTH-EAST SULAWESI Kendari
24. SOUTH KALIMANTAN Banjarmasin
25. SOUTH SULAWESI Makassar
26. SOUTH SUMATRA Palembang
27. WEST JAVA Bandung
28. WEST KALIMANTAN Pontianak
29. WEST NUSA TENGGARA Mataram
30. WEST SUMATRA Padang
31. YOGYAKARTA Yogyakarta

The terraced rice fields of the southern slopes, groaning with abundance, are the dominant feature of the rural landscape and one of the great sights of Bali.

Bali was once heavily forested, but volcanic eruptions have destroyed some of the lowland forest and people have cut down much of the rest. Deciduous forests abound on the drier northern slopes, and the north-western corner of Bali is virtually uninhabited.

The coastline of Bali is ruggedly beautiful and punctuated with enticing, sandy beaches. Southern Bali is famous as a surfers' paradise and famous, too, for the glorious sunsets that can be enjoyed from the beaches.

Bali was dealt a terrible blow in 2002, when terrorist bombs claimed more than 200 lives in the tourist centre of Kuta (see box on pages 94–5).

Most of the Indonesian people who live on Bali are Hindu, unlike in the rest of Indonesia, where the majority of people are Muslim.

Lake Toba and the Batak people

In the heart of the province of Sumatara Utara (North Sumatra) lies the fabled Lake Toba, the largest lake in Southeast Asia with an area of 1140 sq kilometres (440 sq miles). With a depth of around 529 m (1735 ft), the lake is also one of the ten deepest in the world; it is 905 m (2975 ft) above sea level. It was formed about 75,000 years ago when a volcano erupted with unimaginable force and collapsed in on itself. According to some experts, it was the most violent eruption of the last million years. The lake then formed in the collapsed crater.

The lake is surrounded by pine-fringed beaches and steep slopes and cliffs – the sides of the collapsed volcano – that rise to a height of just under 1200 m (4000 ft). After a second mighty volcanic eruption 25,000 years ago, the island of Samosir emerged from the middle of the lake. The island has an area of 640 sq kilometres (250 sq miles).

Lake Toba and its surroundings are one of Indonesia's most famous beauty spots, with good swimming and walking, as well as being the home of one of its most fascinating peoples, the Batak.

The Batak have intrigued Westerners since European missionaries first encountered them at the end of the 18th century. Remarkably, they have managed to preserve their unique culture while at the same time adapting to their relatively recent contact with the wider world of the Indonesian nation. One feature of Batak life has, however, disappeared – the practice of **cannibalism**. The Batak gained great notoriety as reports of their cannibalism filtered back to the West during the 19th century.

The Dutch missionaries converted most of the Batak to Protestant Christianity, although a minority remain Muslim. In both cases, however, the imported religion is combined with earlier Batak traditions, such as ancestor worship.

There are six major Batak groups, and the Toba Batak are most likely to have contact with outsiders. They live around the lake whose name they share and on the island of Samosir.

The most visible features of Toba Batak culture are traditional fabrics and architecture. The traditional Toba Batak house is raised above the ground on stilts anchored on stone bases. The house has a swayback roof, which slopes towards the centre from soaring gables that are richly carved with animals and birds. Buffalo horns adorn the top of the gable at either end of the roof ridge. Traditionally, only wood and rope were used in construction, but today corrugated iron has mostly replaced thatched roofs. The entrance to the living area is a trap door at the top of a flight of steps. As many as a dozen families may share a Toba Batak house.

Gunung Leuser National Park

In 1980, the Indonesian government combined and expanded a number of established wildlife reserves and sanctuaries to create the Gunung Leuser National Park. The park straddles the border between the provinces of North Sumatra and Aceh, extending over an area of some 9500 sq kilometres (3670 sq miles). It is one of the largest as well as one of the most important protected forested areas in Southeast Asia. The nearest large urban centre is Medan (Indonesia's fourth-largest city) in North Sumatra, which is a six-hour bus journey from Ketambe, the principal entrance point to the park.

Walking tracks range from one-day walks to the gruelling 14-day trek to the top of Gunung (Mount) Leuser, one of Sumatra's highest peaks at 3381 m (11,093 ft). The trek passes through virgin rainforest and alpine meadows to ascend the mountain.

Visitors have to have a permit and hire the services of a registered guide to enter the park. Guides build shelters at night, carry the bags, cook food, cut through vegetation on overgrown tracks and show visitors the wildlife.

An exciting way of exploring this great wilderness – one that is especially popular with the young and adventurous – is by rafting down the Sungai Alas (Alas River), which slices through the centre of the park. This trip offers not only the thrills of white-water rafting, but also the opportunity to enjoy the awe-inspiring scenery and to observe many of the park's fascinating plants, animals and birds.

More than 380 species of birds can be found in the park, and there are plenty of **primates** to be seen, such as the white-breasted Thomas's leaf monkey with its prominent crest. The park is also home to a number of endangered mammals, including the Sumatran tiger, the clouded leopard and the Malayan sun bear. Visitors are unlikely to catch a glimpse of these creatures, and even less likely to see one of the 60 or so remaining Sumatran rhinos, which are one of the world's most endangered animals.

There is one endangered species, however, that visitors can be almost guaranteed a glimpse of. On the eastern edge of the park, just outside the village of Bukit Lawang, visitors flock to the famous Orangutan Rehabilitation Centre. The centre was set up in 1973 by two Swiss women and is dedicated to the return of captive and abandoned orangutans to the wild.

Loss of habitat has pushed this delightful primate to the edge of extinction. At the same time, its cuddly image makes it a highly prized pet, especially in Singapore. As cuddly infants and playful youngsters, they have great appeal for their owners.

Unfortunately, like many exotic pets, they lose their appeal when fully grown and are often abandoned. Having been used to being fed and looked after, these orangutans are unable to find food and look after themselves.

If they are lucky, the abandoned orangutans end up at the Rehabilitation Centre. After a period in **quarantine** and a medical check-up, the domesticated orangutans are retrained in basic survival skills, such as climbing trees, finding food and building nests. Then they are set free in the nearby national park and encouraged to fend for themselves. A feeding station provides a nutritious meal of milk and bananas for the newly released orangutans or for those having difficulty finding food in the forest. Feeding time is very popular with visitors, but the centre's workers deliberately keep the food bland and uninteresting to encourage the orangutans to forage for themselves.

Several hundred orangutans have been successfully reintroduced to the park, which now has a total population of about 5000.

An orangutan helps itself to some food at the Rehabilitation Centre. The animals are not encouraged to rely on this source of food.

The lush, green terraced rice fields of Bali are one of the most memorable sights on the island.

Nusa Tenggara

The islands of Nusa Tenggara – which means 'south-eastern islands' – start just to the east of Bali. They are strung out like a series of stepping stones for about 1000 kilometres (620 miles) all the way to the island of Timor. Nusa Tenggara is made up of the major islands of Lombok, Sumbawa, Flores, Sumba and Timor, along with hundreds of smaller islands.

Lombok is a little smaller than Bali and is much less developed than its famous neighbour. In recent years, however, it has been attracting visitors who want to get away from the crowds and are drawn by the island's long stretches of empty, white sand beaches.

Lombok is dominated by the dormant volcano Gunung Rinjani, which, at a height of 3726 metres (12,224 feet), is the third-highest mountain in Indonesia; the highest is Puncak Jaya in Papua. Trekkers head for the crater rim to gaze at the beautiful turquoise lake, Segara Anak (Child of the Sea), within. The main volcano last erupted in 1901, but in 1994, one of its secondary craters erupted, raising fears that Rinjani may only be sleeping.

With their terraced rice fields, the southern slopes of Rinjani and the fertile central plain below are reminiscent of Bali. Generally, though, the island is less lush because it gets significantly less rainfall. In the far south and east, Lombok is quite barren and suffers drought and searing heat during the dry season (May–October).

Next in the chain is Sumbawa, which is about the size of Bali and Lombok together. The landscape is very rugged and the climate is dry and hot. Sumbawa has been described as a moonscape, and there is certainly nothing at all to compare with the lush green of Bali.

Rice is grown in flooded paddy fields in the fertile central plain of Lombok.

Sumbawa has its own stark beauty, though, and the west coast provides beautiful beaches with good surf. The northern part of the island is dominated by Mount Tambora, whose massive eruption over several days in July 1815 had a worldwide effect. The ash particles and other debris circled the globe, blocking out some of the Sun's rays, which caused the summer of 1816 to be one of the coldest on record. Like the eruption of Krakatau nearly 70 years later, Mount Tambora's eruption provided the world with some spectacular sunsets.

For most visitors, Sumbawa is usually seen as a way of getting from Lombok to one of Indonesia's great tourist draws, the island of Komodo off the east coast. Komodo is a national park and home to the famous Komodo dragon (see box on page 31).

Deer Island

Bali Barat National Park extends over nearly 770 sq kilometres (300 sq miles) on the western tip of Bali. It ranges from the dry northern shore through wooded slopes and central **savannah** to the rainforests and mangrove swamps of the south. Most of the park is closed to visitors, and even where tracks are open, visitors must have a permit and be accompanied by an official guide.

Just off the north coast is the uninhabited Pulau Menjangan (Deer Island). It is an exceptionally beautiful spot, home to the rare Java deer – from which it takes its name – as well as monkeys, **civets** and the very rare wild Javan buffalo. The island also has a great variety of bird life, including one of the rarest birds in the world, the Bali white mina, or Bali starling. This beautiful little white bird, with black-tipped wings and a brilliant blue mask around its eyes, numbers only a few dozen at most in the wild. Attempts are being made to reintroduce captive birds – of which there are several thousand in zoos around the world – into the wild.

While Deer Island is administered by the national park, visitors are permitted to take a boat across to it without a guide. It is, in fact, the most visited part of the national park because it is surrounded by spectacular coral reefs and has the best diving (snorkelling and scuba) around Bali. The visibility is superb – up to 50 m (165 ft) – with spectacular cliffs, caves and a wealth of colourful tropical fish.

Beyond Komodo Island lies Flores, which, for many people, is the most beautiful in the chain of islands that make up Nusa Tenggara. Certainly, it is one of the finest beauty spots in all of Indonesia, and torrential seasonal rainfall gives it a green lushness that its nearest neighbours lack. The island is 368 kilometres (230 miles) long, but not more than 75 kilometres (45 miles) across. Because of its slinky shape, a local name for Flores translates as 'Serpent Island'. A great ridge made up of fifteen volcanoes runs along the centre of the island. A reminder of how the Ring of Fire brings earthquakes as well as volcanic eruptions came in 1992, when an earthquake in eastern Flores killed 1500 people.

Sumba, to the south of Flores and between Sumbawa and Timor, lies outside the Ring of Fire. In contrast to all its volcanic neighbours, this oval-shaped island consists of rolling hills and plateaux. East Sumba is drier while west Sumba gets plenty of rainfall and is therefore much greener. At one time, Sumba was famed

The caldera (or layers of ash) of the volcano Kelimutu on the island of Flores contains three lakes that are coloured different shades of blues and browns. Minerals in the water mean that the colours change over the years.

Timor has rocky soils and is dotted with plantar palms. Along the north coast, the mountains sweep right down to the sea.

for its sandalwood and was known as the 'Sandalwood Isle', but today there is little of that fragrant wood left standing in the island's forests.

At 480 kilometres (300 miles) long and 80 kilometres (50 miles) wide, Timor is by far the largest of the islands of Nusa Tenggara. Only the western half of the island is part of Indonesia – East Timor gained its independence in 2002. Like Sumba, it is not volcanic, but Timor is still very mountainous, with a spine of peaks running the whole length of the island. Much of the landscape is starkly beautiful, but in recent years, Timor's many attractions have been completely overshadowed by political turmoil and violence (see box on page 78).

The provinces of Kalimantan

Indonesia shares the huge island of Borneo with Malaysia and the **sultanate** of Brunei. With an area of 755,000 square kilometres (292,000 square miles), Borneo is the third-largest island in the world (after Greenland and New Guinea). Just under three-quarters of it belong to Indonesia, as the four provinces of West, Central, South and East Kalimantan.

The island is a sparsely populated land of swamps, jungle, rivers and mountains. The Kalimantan lowland rainforest has been severely damaged and depleted by logging, mining and drilling for oil. Forest fires, too, have taken a terrible toll in recent years.

One of the prime attractions of Kalimantan is Tanjung Puting National Park, a beautiful stretch of forest and swamp teeming with wildlife. Within the park is a well-known orangutan rehabilitation centre, established in the 1970s to help abandoned pet orangutans to readjust to life in the wild.

When European explorers and later colonists came across Borneo's **indigenous** people, the Dayaks, they were horrified to find that they were head-hunters. This gave Borneo a lurid and sensational image that persisted long after the Dutch stamped out the practice.

The mighty Komodo dragon

Komodo Island and its neighbours, including, Flores and Rinca are home to one of the most unusual-looking creatures on the Earth – the Komodo dragon. Sometimes referred to as a 'living dinosaur', the Komodo dragon is the largest species of monitor lizard. The name 'monitor' comes from folklore that says that these giant lizards track or 'monitor' crocodiles in order to scavenge from their kills.

Because of its very restricted habitat, the Komodo dragon was completely unknown to Westerners until 1910. Heavily protected, their numbers are a healthy 5000 or so and rising. About half live on Komodo Island. The whole island is a national park devoted to the lizards' conservation and to the flourishing trade in tourists who come to see these extraordinary reptiles.

The largest Komodo dragon ever recorded measured just over 3 m (10 ft) from tail to snout and weighed in at a reported 166 kg (365 lb). More commonly, males are about 2.6 m (8½ ft) long and weigh about 90 kg (200 lb). Females are about two-thirds that size.

Even at these smaller sizes, however, Komodo dragons are fearsome predators. They have powerful jaws and jagged, serrated teeth that can slice their prey to ribbons. These conventional weapons are combined with a long, whip-like tail that the dragon lashes from side to side as it sprints after and attacks prey.

Komodo dragons have enormous appetites and can consume nearly their own body weight of meat in a day. They devour mainly carrion (dead animals) but also kill deer, goats, rodents and monkeys. On one occasion they killed and ate an elderly Swiss tourist.

The myth that Komodo dragons have a poisonous bite – or even poisonous breath – probably results from the fact that their bites rapidly become infected. They patiently follow wounded prey until the infected bite has weakened the victim sufficiently to make the kill easy.

The island of Sulawesi

To the east of Kalimantan is the K-shaped island of Sulawesi, with its four peninsulas separated by three deep gulfs. The island was previously known as Celebes. 'Sulawesi' means 'Island of Iron', in recognition of the rich seams of nickel and iron ore mined there.

Sulawesi has a land area of 189,000 square kilometres (73,000 square miles), although it occupies a considerably greater area if the gulfs between the peninsulas are included. It is divided into the four provinces of South, South-east, Central and North Sulawesi.

At Sulawesi's core is a group of eleven volcanic mountains. In the past, these mountains have isolated the four peninsulas from each other because they make overland communications so difficult. Even within the peninsulas, it can be difficult to get around because almost everywhere the ground rises steeply from a narrow coastal fringe.

The centre of Sulawesi is dominated by volcanic highlands that effectively cut off the four peninsulas from one another.

The Maluku archipelago

Maluku is an archipelago comprising more than 1000 islands. In the past, it was known as the Moluccas, and long ago, it was known as the fabled Spice Islands. Chinese, Arab and later European explorers and traders in the 16th century came to the islands of Maluku in search of spices, such as mace, nutmeg and cloves, which grew only on these islands. Maluku was the first part of Indonesia to have contact with the new arrivals from the other side of the world.

The islands of Maluku are scattered over the triangle of sea that lies between Sulawesi, Papua and Timor. They are divided into the provinces of Maluku and North Maluku. The most northerly and southerly of the islands are separated by a distance of more than 1000 kilometres (620 miles). Large, inhabited islands such as Seram, Buru and Halmahera are greatly outnumbered by hundreds of uninhabited little **atoll**s, the peaks of submerged volcanoes. Maluku is right in the middle of

This nutmeg plantation is on one of the Banda Islands, which are part of Maluku. The hard seed of the tree is grated to make the spice nutmeg and the outer seed covering produces mace.

the Ring of Fire, and its history has been regularly punctuated by volcanic eruptions. The sea is very deep here, reaching a depth of more than 4900 metres (16,000 feet) in a trench south-east of Halmahera.

The northern and central islands offer beautiful wild landscapes, with dense rainforests and mountainous interiors fringed by white beaches. The interiors of many of these islands remain unknown to outsiders. Southern Maluku is drier than the north, the landscape is more arid and, because of its remoteness, it remains an Indonesian backwater.

Papua

The island of New Guinea – the second largest in the world after Greenland – is divided between the country of Papua New Guinea, in the east, and the Indonesian province of Papua, in the west, known until 2001 as Irian Jaya. Vast swathes of Papua are wilderness – perhaps the last place on Earth where the modern world has failed to intrude. Experts believe that there are tribes in the rainforest who have had no contact with the outside world.

Papua covers an area of 410,000 square kilometres (150,000 square miles). A central range of non-volcanic mountains includes Puncak Jaya – at 5030 metres (16,503 feet), the highest in Indonesia. To the north lie more mountain ranges, while to the south, virtually impenetrable rainforest eventually gives way to coastal mangrove swamps.

CLIMATE

The Indonesian archipelago has an **equatorial** climate, which means that there are only two seasons – a rainy season from November to April and a drier season from

Maros caves

A series of caves about 40 kilometres (25 miles) north-east of Makassar in Sulawesi contain some of the earliest art in Indonesia. Together, the caves and the surrounding landscape are a beautiful park, which is delightful for walking in, and some of the caves are easily accessible. The prehistoric paintings are thought to be at least 5000 years old, including handprints and paintings of deer and wild pigs. They have been compared to the famous paintings of wild animals found in caves at Lascaux in France.

May to October. The pattern of rainfall is determined by two **monsoons,** a north-east monsoon that pushes in wet air and a south-west monsoon that pushes in dry air.

Close to the equator, however, there is little variation in rainfall throughout the year, so the distinction between rainy and dry seasons means little here. To add to the confusion, in the most northerly parts of Indonesia – in northern Sumatra and North Maluku – the wet–dry pattern tends to be reversed. In addition, local conditions create countless microclimates – climates contained within a small area. So while it is true to say that the annual rainfall in Indonesia generally exceeds 190 centimetres (75 inches), in many cases that paints a false picture. In Manado in north-east Sulawesi,

A river winds through the flat mangrove swamps near the coast of Asmat, in Papua. The flow of the water changes direction every time the tide comes in.

Birds of paradise

In 1522, the Spanish ship *Victoria* arrived at Seville in Spain having completed the first circumnavigation of the world. Among the many wonders collected ashore were five bird skins that simply astonished those who saw them. Purchased in the Maluku islands, the skins were fabulously feathered and, for reasons unknown, the legs had been removed, which led European observers to conclude that the birds spent their entire lives airborne.

It would be several centuries before this myth was exploded. In the meantime, however, the beauty of the birds and the fact that they apparently never touched down on earth resulted in their being given the heavenly name 'birds of paradise'.

There are 43 species of birds of paradise distributed naturally throughout the islands of Indonesia, Papua New Guinea and Australia. The 30 species found in Indonesia include the famous greater bird of paradise and the very rare king bird of paradise.

The males sport spectacular plumage for courtship, but it has sadly proved a burden for these exotic creatures. For centuries there was a demand for the plumage in Asia, but worse was to come. During the late 19th century, women's hats decorated with bird of paradise feathers became fashionable in the West. An estimated 50,000 birds were slaughtered for that purpose. Even today, although the birds are protected, there is a flourishing illegal trade in bird skins.

The king bird of paradise is a rare species that is found in parts of Indonesia.

for example, rainfall is nearly twice the average, while at Palu in the centre of the island, it is just over half. In the western foothills of the Barisan mountain range in Sumatra, there are places where the annual rainfall averages 610 centimetres (240 inches). Overall, Indonesia is always hot and often oppressively humid, but it is a little cooler during the rainy season.

While rainfall patterns vary, temperatures are quite constant. The daily average minimum and maximum temperatures hardly vary at all during the year, and never by more than a degree or two. They range from 21° C (70° F) to 32° C (90° F), although it can be much cooler in the mountains.

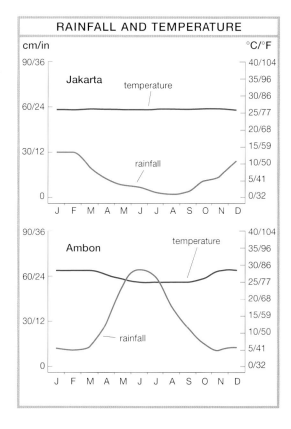

PLANTS AND ANIMALS

Indonesia has the greatest variety of plant and animal species in Southeast Asia and – according to some criteria – in the world. The islands comprise only 1.3 per cent of the Earth's land surface, yet are estimated to contain 17 per cent of all the world's species. This figure includes 12 per cent of mammals, 17 per cent of birds, 16 per cent of reptiles and amphibians, 25 per cent of fish and 10 per cent of flowering plants. A large percentage of species in all these categories can be found only in Indonesia.

Biological zones

The unique character of Indonesia's wildlife and plants results from the archipelago's position between Asia and Australia. This has resulted in there being three

The temperature in different parts of Indonesia varies little over the year. Rainfall can vary greatly, however. Ambon, in Maluku, has a much wetter rainy season than the capital, Jakarta. While the rainy season occurs from November to April in most parts of the country, in Ambon the wettest part of the year is between April and September.

These fields contain sweet potatoes, grown by the Dani people of Papua as the staple food of the region. Papua shares many plant and wildlife species with Australia.

biological zones within the country's borders. Western Indonesia from Sumatra to Bali was joined to the Asian mainland during early Ice Ages, when sea levels were much lower. This meant that Oriental species migrated to those islands. Similarly, eastern Indonesia from Papua to the eastern part of the Maluku archipelago was linked to Australia, so Australasian species migrated there. Central Indonesia – Nusa Tenggara, Sulawesi and western Maluku – is an area of overlap. This biological zone is called Wallacea in honour of the British **naturalist** Alfred Russel Wallace (1823–1913), who first drew attention to the divisions (see box on page 42).

Endangered mammals

Northern Sumatra and western Java are home to large mammals whose numbers dwindle and disappear completely farther east. Some of these magnificent animals, such as the Sumatran tiger, the clouded leopard and both Sumatran and Javan species of rhinos, are extremely endangered.

The Rockefeller mystery

In 1961, Michael Rockefeller, the 23-year-old son of US Governor Rockefeller of New York and heir to a vast fortune, mounted an expedition to study and photograph the little-known Ndani peoples of the Papua central highlands. Having completed their work, Rockefeller and his companion, Rene Wassing, explored further south, and were astounded by the quality of primitive art they found in the Asmat swamps, along the Betsj River where it enters the Afarura Sea.

Rockefeller was determined to acquire some of this unknown work for the New York Museum of Primitive Art, and later in the year he and Wassing made their way by canoe down the coast to the Betsj River. However, heavy seas capsized their flimsy craft, and while their two Asmat guides swam for shore, Rockefeller and Wassing clung to the upturned canoe all night. At dawn, Rockefeller decided to swim for shore

to get help, and left Wassing with the words 'I think I can make it'. She never saw him again. Wassing was rescued, and the massive – unsuccessful – air-sea search led by Governor Rockefeller made headlines around the world.

Seven years later, a report reached Milt Machlin, the editor of an American adventure magazine, that someone claiming to be Michael Rockefeller had been seen in a remote part of New Guinea, far from where he disappeared and apparently held captive by a cannibal tribe. Machlin mounted an expedition to get to the bottom of the mystery, but found no trace of the missing explorer.

Rockefeller may simply have drowned, or a shark or crocodile, both plentiful in those waters, may have taken him. But from the beginning there were rumours that Rockefeller had been unlucky enough to fall into the hands of cannibals – rumours that have never been dispelled.

While visitors are unlikely ever to see these rare creatures in the wild, there is a wealth of wildlife to be enjoyed in Sumatra's Gunung Leuser National Park (see page 24) and Java's Ujung Kulon National Park (see page 20). Sumatra is the home of Indonesia's largest mammal, the Asian elephant, and of the orangutan, which can be seen in the semi-wild at a special reserve near the village of Bukit Lawang (see page 24). Sumatra and Java also have wild populations of other primates including macaques and gibbons.

Wasur National Park

New Guinea and Australia were only totally separated by water about 8000 years ago, which in geological time, is little more than the blinking of an eye. This means that Wasur National Park, which borders the Papua New Guinean Tonda Reserve, not only resembles the northern Australia that it was once attached to, but it shares a host of the same species. There are kangaroos and wallabies, along with that well-known Australian bird, the laughing kookaburra (a large member of the kingfisher family).

Birds are a great feature of the park, with 491 recorded species, some of which are found nowhere else. There are many other fascinating creatures to be seen, including the short-beaked **echidna**, which is related to the Australian duck-billed **platypus**.

Wallacea

The central islands that make up the Wallacea zone are famous for their bird life, including hornbills, egrets, herons and kingfishers. The occasional sighting of **cockatoos** makes the Australian connection apparent. The island of Sulawesi marks the furthest westwards range of Australian **marsupials**, in the form of **possums**. As well as a mix of Oriental and Australasian species, this region is home to one of the most unusual creatures on the Earth – the Komodo dragon (see box on page 31).

Australasian species

It is in Papua, at the eastern end of the Indonesian archipelago, that the Australian influence is so pronounced. Wallabies and tree kangaroos along with marsupial mice make their home here. There are more than 700 species of birds known to breed in this rainforest wilderness, including 26 species of the wildly plumaged birds of paradise and the large flightless **cassowary**.

A wealth of plant life

The archipelago's vegetation varies according to rainfall, altitude and soil condition. About 60 per cent of Indonesia is covered with tropical rainforest, including much of Kalimantan and almost all of Papua. This, and the fact that most of the plant species originate from the Asian mainland, give Indonesia a remarkably rich and diverse plant life.

There are an estimated 40,000 different plant species belonging to 3000 different families. The plant species found in Indonesia include 5000 species of orchid, ranging in size from the majestic tiger orchid – the largest in the world – to tiny edible species that are believed to have medicinal properties. These orchids are just one example of the thousands of plants that are used in the preparation of traditional herbal medicines, an important feature of Indonesian life.

The world's largest flowers

Sumatra is home to the world's largest flower, the foul-smelling rafflesia, named after the British colonial administrator Sir Thomas Stamford Raffles (1781– 1826) who found one in the early 19th century. Like something out of science fiction, the lurid red rafflesia bloom is about 1 metre (3 feet) across and weighs up to 9 kilograms (20 pounds). It smells of rotten meat and attracts carrion flies, which help to pollinate the plant.

Also found in Sumatra is a rare giant lily that grows almost as large as the rafflesia. Just as exotic is the carnivorous pitcher plant, which feeds on insects.

The future of the rainforest

Indonesia is home to 3000 species of trees, which include sandalwood as well as many valuable rainforest hardwoods. Deforestation on a devastating scale threatens the future of the rainforest and, with it, the environment of Southeast Asia. More immediately, it threatens the habitat of many of the world's most endangered species.

The tiger orchid, which grows in Indonesia, is the largest orchid species in the world.

The Wallace line

Alfred Russel Wallace was a Welsh naturalist who spent eight years exploring Indonesia from 1854 to 1862. He collected over 100,000 specimens, which greatly increased knowledge about this little-known region of the world. In the course of his expedition, Wallace was struck by the differences between similar animals from one island to another. He also noted the astounding differences between the Oriental species of the western islands and such obviously Australian species as kangaroos and other marsupials in the eastern islands.

Independent of the naturalist Charles Darwin, who was his friend and contemporary, Wallace arrived at the conclusion we now know as the theory of evolution, which explains how species adapt and change over time in response to their environment. Wallace believed that there was a fundamental division between Bali and Lombok, however narrow the waters between the two. His evidence was that very many Asian species – most noticeably the great mammals such as tigers, elephants and rhinos – did not extend east of Java and Bali. Similarly, Australian marsupials appeared at the eastern end of the archipelago but not further west. He drew a line, the Wallace line, between what he called the Indo-Malayan and Austro-Malayan regions. The line ran north–south between Borneo and Sulawesi, and Bali and Lombok. In later years, Wallace changed his mind about Sulawesi and moved it into the Austro-Malayan camp.

In the 20th century, it was accepted that, with so much overlap, a third central region – Wallacea – was needed to explain the mixed wildlife of the central islands of Indonesia.

JAKARTA

Jakarta is the largest city and the capital of Indonesia. There may have been a Hindu settlement on the site of the present-day city as early as the 5th century. In the 12th century, the port of Sunda Kelapa was established on this swampy location by the Sundanese kingdom of Pajarjaran. Under the Pajarjarans, a Hindu people whose kingdom was centred in western Java, the port flourished for more than three centuries. In 1513, however, the first Europeans arrived at Sunda Kelapa – Portuguese explorers in search of spices. Nine years later, the Portuguese turned up again, this time signing a friendship treaty with the Pajarjarans and establishing a trading post. Shortly after, in 1527, Sunda Kelapa was conquered by the **Muslim** sultanate of Demak, based on Java's north coast. The port was renamed Jayakerta, which means 'Glorious Fortress'. The anniversary of the day of victory, 22 June, is celebrated as marking the birth of Jakarta.

By the early 17th century, the Dutch had replaced the Portuguese as the major European presence in the region, and in 1610, they established a trading post at Jayakerta. Relations between the Dutch and their Muslim hosts soon became strained and English traders got involved in trying to help push out the Dutch. This led to disaster when, in 1619, a Dutch fleet burned Jayakerta to the ground (see page 61).

The Dutch built a new town and called it Batavia, which became the property of the Dutch East India Company (see page 59). Batavia was a flourishing Dutch outpost during the 17th century, featuring fine

A few reminders of the old Dutch town of Batavia remain in modern-day Jakarta, including these Dutch colonial buildings in the Kota district.

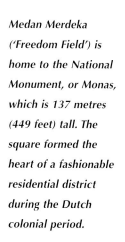

Medan Merdeka ('Freedom Field') is home to the National Monument, or Monas, which is 137 metres (449 feet) tall. The square formed the heart of a fashionable residential district during the Dutch colonial period.

civic buildings and canals reminiscent of Amsterdam. It gained the grand description of 'Queen of the East', but by the 18th century, Batavia was in decline. It was dubbed the 'White Man's Graveyard' because of the terrible toll taken by the diseases cholera and malaria.

After a brief period of British occupation in the early 19th century, the Dutch re-established control of Batavia and set about draining the swamps and canals that had proved such a breeding ground for disease. Before long, yet another phrase to describe the city gained currency, 'Pearl of the Orient'.

Batavia remained in Dutch hands until World War Two (1939–45), but in March 1942, it was occupied by the Japanese, who renamed it Jakarta, a shortened version of its old name. After the war, the Dutch briefly returned, but in 1949 after an armed conflict they stepped aside for the creation of the new republic of Indonesia, with Jakarta as its capital.

Today, the city is administered as a separate special district with about 8.4 million inhabitants. The sprawling suburbs bring the total up to around 12.5 million. The Indonesian motto is 'Unity in diversity', and the streets of Jakarta certainly teem with people representing Indonesia's ethnic diversity.

Much of central Jakarta looks like any other major city, with towering office blocks competing for space with big international hotels. The most interesting area of Jakarta is Kota, north of the centre and the centre of old Batavia. While much Dutch colonial architecture was destroyed by the Japanese or knocked down during the postwar building boom, fine examples remain to give a flavour of the 'Pearl of the Orient'.

Modern Jakarta is a bustling city that is home to millions of people. Although there is much wealth in the capital, it also has the worst slums in the country. Gunung Gede, an active volcano, can be seen here in the distance.

YOGYAKARTA

Yogya, as it is usually abbreviated, is not one of Java's largest cities, but it lays proud claim to being Java's cultural heart. Situated in central Java, Yogya is home to the prestigious Indonesian Fine Arts Institute and is a magnet for Indonesian artists and performers. There are many music and dance schools, and all the classical Javanese arts such as dance, drama, poetry and puppet shows are performed to a high standard. Yogya is one of the best places to enjoy the unique sound of the famous **gamelan** orchestras. The city is also noted for producing batik textiles of the highest quality (see box on page 92).

Yogya's greatest attraction is the *kraton*, a walled city within a city that was the palace compound of Yogya's sultans. Built in the 18th century, the *kraton* houses not only the sumptuous palace but also a mosque, two museums and a maze of streets and courtyards filled with craft workshops and fascinating markets. More than 25,000 people live within the compound.

One of the most important streets in Yogya is Jalan A Yani, which joins the railway station to the north with the old walled city named the Kraton.

CENTRAL YOGYAKARTA

Another attraction of Yogya is that two of Indonesia's greatest ancient monuments are located nearby. Sixteen kilometres (10 miles) north-east of the city lies the Prambanan Plain. A huge complex of Hindu temples was erected here more than 1000 years ago (see page 53). Much of it is buried, but the elaborately ornate ruins, much restored, are the most extensive in Indonesia.

Yogya's bird market is located near the kraton. Many different bird species can be bought and sold here, including pigeons, which are a favourite with Yogya residents.

About 40 kilometres (25 miles) north-west of Yogya, in a spectacular volcanic setting, is one of the world's astounding constructions – Borobudur (see page 53). It is the largest of all Buddhist temples and the biggest ancient monument south of the equator. Begun in the 7th century and built over hundreds of years – centuries before the great cathedrals of Europe – Borobudur is 45.7 metres (150 feet) high and contains a million blocks of volcanic rock. The gigantic temple is decorated with 1460 relief panels inscribed with the Buddha's teachings, as well as another 1212 ornamental panels that provide a fascinating picture of Javanese life at the time.

Past and present

*'One nation – Indonesia; one people – Indonesian;
one language – Indonesian.'*

Nationalist sentiment given voice by the All Indonesia Youth Congress, 1928

Indonesia is at the cutting edge of two important debates about human evolution: the origin of modern humans and the date when modern humans left Africa for Asia and Europe. In 1891, the Dutch **palaeontologist** Eugene Dubois uncovered a prehistoric skull and other fragments of early human-like bones in central Java. Dubois startled the world when he announced that he had found the 'missing link' – that is, the ape-like human who was descended from a distant prehuman ancestor and who, in turn, was the ancestor of modern humans. 'Java Man', as Dubois' discovery became popularly known, was an overnight sensation (see box on page 50). If Dubois' assertion was correct, it proved that humans had indeed evolved in the distant past from a prehuman ancestor.

Java Man, which was given the scientific name *Homo erectus*, was dated to between 500,000 and a million years ago. Since then, the discovery of similar fossil remains in Africa have pushed the date of *Homo erectus*'s emergence back to over 1.8 million years ago. Although most palaeontologists believe that Africa was *Homo erectus*'s ancestral home, Java Man is still the oldest early human ever discovered outside Africa.

More recently, about 40,000 years ago, modern humans (*Homo sapiens sapiens*) began to make an appearance in the islands. They arrived in the west and

This 1719 engraving shows European vessels at Gammalamme, a port in the Moluccas that was an important base for the spice trade with the West.

FACT FILE

● Outside Africa, which is accepted as the cradle of humanity, Indonesia has the world's earliest-known prehistory.

● Christopher Columbus was heading for the Spice Islands on his famous voyage of 1492, when he reached America by accident.

● The Dutch were the major power in Indonesia for 350 years, but they were not able to impose their authority over the whole of the archipelago until the dying days of their colonial empire in the 1940s.

● Early Indonesians were animists – they believed that all objects had a soul.

Is Java Man older than we think?

Java Man – a reconstruction of which is shown here – has been surrounded by controversy ever since his discovery. Dubois seemed to have differing views about just how human he really was. And creationists (who do not believe the theory of evolution) reject the whole idea of a 'missing link' between the human race and an ape-like ancestor.

Recently, new dating techniques have suggested that Java Man may be a million years older than his estimated age of 500,000 to a million years. That would mean he lived almost at the same time as the earliest *Homo erectus* fossils found in Africa. The validity of these findings is hotly disputed. In any case, they do not contradict the belief that *Homo erectus* evolved in Africa. It would mean, however, that he did not wait a million years before migrating eastwards to Southeast Asia.

north from mainland Asia and in the south and east from Australia, taking advantage of temporary land bridges created by the much lower sea levels during the last Ice Age. Then, around the end of the Ice Age some 12,000 to 15,000 years ago, newcomers began arriving from the Asian mainland.

PREHISTORIC PEOPLES

Like others elsewhere in the world, these prehistoric peoples would have existed as hunter-gatherers for thousands of years. Later, they would have developed agriculture and lived in settled communities. This would have happened at widely differing times in different places, but it is thought that pockets of settled agriculture were in existence by 2000 BC. Rice cultivation was exceptionally well suited to the nutrient-rich volcanic soils of Java and Bali. Growing rice success-fully requires people to co-operate and work together, which encouraged the development of villages. With village life, people's relationships with each other became increasingly complex, and alliances were created with nearby communities.

Trade between islands followed, and by the 2nd century AD, trade links were being established between the western islands and Southeast Asia, India and, later, China. The Indian influence was of great significance because it brought **Hinduism** and, later, **Buddhism**.

The oldest evidence of a Hindu civilization in Indonesia comes from Kutei in eastern Kalimantan. Stone inscriptions, written in Sanskrit (an ancient Indian language) and dating from the early 5th century, have been found here. At about the same time, the earli-est-known Hindu kingdom appeared in western Java.

Hinduism, once introduced, rapidly took hold, and by the 5th and 6th centuries, small Hindu kingdoms were dotted around the Indonesian archipelago. This was the beginning of a 1000-year period of Indian influ-ence, both Hindu and Buddhist.

INDONESIA'S CLASSICAL AGE

Beginning in the 7th century, powerful dynasties began to emerge, first in Sumatra and then in more heavily populated Java. This so-called Classical Age of Indonesian history began with the great Buddhist kingdom of Srivijaya, whose capital was Palembang on the Musi River in south-east Sumatra.

The Srivijaya kingdom

Palembang's strategic position gave Srivijaya control of the Strait of Malaka between Sumatra and the Malay peninsula and the Sunda Strait between Sumatra and Java. Palembang is first mentioned in the writings of a Chinese Buddhist traveller who visited in AD 671 and praised it as a seat of learning and religion.

Indonesia had a strategic position on the sea route between China and India. This meant that by the 2nd century AD, trade with these two large Asian civilizations was well established.

THE CLASSICAL KINGDOMS OF INDONESIA

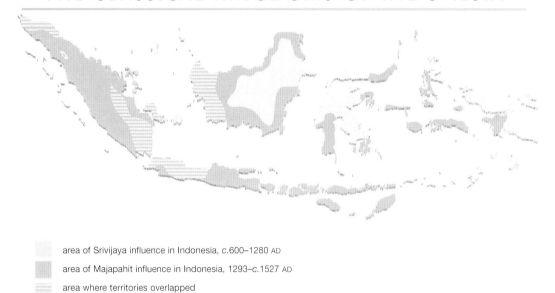

area of Srivijaya influence in Indonesia, *c.*600–1280 AD

area of Majapahit influence in Indonesia, 1293–*c.*1527 AD

area where territories overlapped

Srivijaya was the first kingdom of a Classical Age that endured some 600 years until the decline of the Majapahit kingdom in the 15th century.

A century later, Srivijaya had a more daunting reputation as the dominant maritime power in Southeast Asia, ruling Sumatra, western Java, eastern Borneo and the Malay peninsula as far as southern Thailand (see map above). Its maritime superiority gave Srivijaya almost complete control over trade in the region, which lasted for nearly four centuries. The kingdom was finally overthrown in the 13th century and disappeared virtually without trace.

The Sailendra dynasty

While the Srivijaya held sway in Sumatra and beyond its shores, a mighty kingdom was emerging in nearby Java. This was the Sailendra **dynasty** of central Java. The name 'Sailendra' means 'King of the Mountain', which was the title of the kings of Funan in Vietnam, from whom the Javan royal family claimed descent. Like the Srivijaya, the Sailendra were Buddhist, and they, too, played a part in the lively east–west trade that flowed through Southeast Asia.

The power of the Sailendra kingdom, however, was based on its great agricultural wealth. During its ascendancy from the mid-8th to the mid-10th centuries, the dynasty ruled the eastern two-thirds of Java, as well as Bali, Lombok, some coastal areas of Kalimantan, southern Sulawesi and, for a time, extended as far as Vietnam and Cambodia. Whereas the Srivijaya left nothing of note to be remembered by, the Sailendra legacy includes the magnificent Borobudur temple complex in central Java, which predates and influenced the famous temple of Angkor Wat in Cambodia.

The Sanjaya dynasty

Not far from Borobudur, another central Javanese dynasty rose to power at about this time – the Hindu Sanjaya dynasty. The Sanjaya kingdom disputed

The walls on the terraces of the Buddhist temple Borobudur are covered with beautifully carved relief panels. The temple in central Java is a unique Buddhist monument.

Gajah Mada

During the great days of the Majapahit kingdom, the Indonesian archipelago was, at least to some extent, unified under its powerful kings. It was unified in a way that it had never been before and would not be again until the 20th century. The man credited with achieving so much for the kingdom, and an Indonesian national hero, is Gajah Mada.

Gajah Mada apparently rose from humble beginnings to become a powerful minister serving King Jayanagara (ruled 1309–28). He saved the king from a rebellion in 1319. Far from showing gratitude, however, Jayanagara insulted the proud Gajah Mada by claiming his wife. In 1328, when the king was in need of surgery, Gajah Mada persuaded the surgeon to let the knife slip, which brought Jayanagara's reign to an abrupt end.

Gajah Mada then loyally served Jayanagara's successor, his daughter Tribhuvana, throughout her reign (1328–50), taking every opportunity to expand the kingdom's influence and power. In 1343, he brought Bali back under Majapahit control.

When Tribhuvana's son Hayam Wuruk came to the throne, the young ruler found an immensely able and experienced ally in the older man. In 1351, Gajah Mada ruthlessly suppressed the neighbouring Javanese kingdom of Sunda, which brought a long period of peace. During this time, temple-building and Javanese art and literature flourished. When Gajah Mada died in 1364, Hayam Wuruk had to appoint four successors to handle the great administrator's workload.

Indonesia's first university, established in 1946, is named in Gajah Mada's honour.

Srivijayan maritime dominance, and at the beginning of the 11th century, they were bloodily defeated by their Buddhist rivals. By then, the Sanjayas had created their great monument for posterity, the magnificent Hindu shrine on the Prambanan Plain in Java.

The Majapahit dynasty

Other short-lived kingdoms rose and fell in Java over the next few hundred years. For reasons unknown, the centre of gravity shifted from central to eastern Java. Then, in 1292, the last and greatest of the Javanese kingdoms emerged – the Majapahit dynasty. The capital was at Trowulan, 35 kilometres (22 miles) south-west of Surabaya in east Java. The scale and extent of the archaeological remains at Trowulan give some indication of the wealth and power of their kingdom.

The Majapahits were the controlling influence, if not the outright ruling power, in Sumatra, Bali, the islands of Nusa Tenggara, parts of Borneo and Malaya. They reached their peak during the second half of the 14th century, during the reign of their greatest king, Hayam Wuruk, from 1350 to 1389. This was Java's Golden Age, when a unique blend of Buddhist and Hindu culture made the kingdom of Majapahit admired throughout Southeast Asia.

THE MUSLIM ASCENDANCY

Beginning around 1400, the kingdom of Majapahit went into steady decline, accelerated by the arrival of a dynamic new religious and cultural force in the Indonesian archipelago. For hundreds of years, traders

The relief panels at the Buddhist temple of Borobudur in Java depict tales from the life of the Buddha, as well as scenes from everyday Javanese life.

from Islamic Arabia and the Middle East had had contact with Sumatra and Java – the islands most connected with the east–west trade routes. By the 14th century, Muslim trading states were appearing along the west coast of northern Sumatra. Even while the Majapahits were becoming more poweful, this Muslim presence was advancing steadily down the west coast of Sumatra and then into northern and western Java.

In 1478, internal feuds destroyed the Majapahit kingdom, which fell to the Muslim state of Demak, on Java's west coast. The last Hindu prince and his entourage fled to Bali, which had long been dominated by the Majapahit kingdom. He proclaimed himself king of Bali and encouraged his former subjects in east Java to join him on this Hindu island. Many did so, and today, the effects of this Hindu migration to Bali can still be seen in Balinese cultural and religious life.

The gradual extension of Muslim influence in the islands, especially pronounced in Sumatra and Java, coincided with the first arrival of the Europeans.

This woman is selling herbs and spices at a market in Lombok. Spices were what first attracted foreign traders, including Europeans, to the islands of Indonesia.

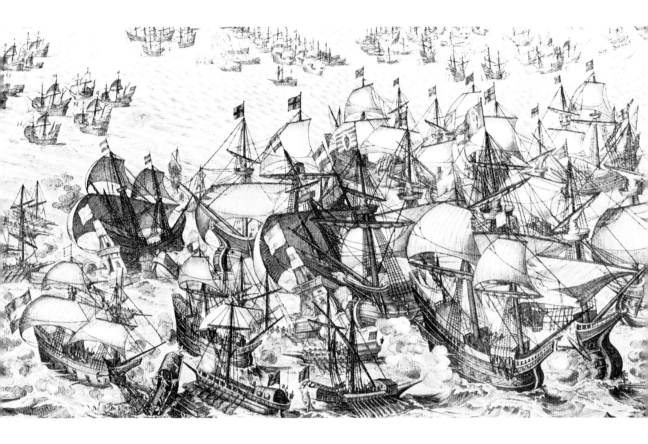

THE ARRIVAL OF THE EUROPEANS

For centuries, Europeans had been in contact with the East, but this contact had been conducted at a distance. Precious goods from Asia were prized by Europeans, and there was a lively trade controlled at the western end by the Italian city-state of Venice. However, the trade was firmly in the control of Asians and Arabs who made the long overland journey along the Silk Road, which connected China with the eastern Mediterranean.

A trade route extended south to the Moluccas, as Maluku was known at the time. These islands were the source of exotic spices that were worth their weight in gold in medieval Europe. Pepper, nutmeg and mace, cinnamon, cloves – all standard ingredients today, but at that time impossible to obtain anywhere except the Moluccas. Towards the end of the 15th century, Portuguese and Spanish seafarers began trying to sail

This print depicts the Dutch taking the port of Banten, in Java, in the late 17th century. Banten is now just a small fishing village, but it was once a major maritime trading centre.

57

The Spice Islands myth

In the 16th century, Europeans believed that spice plants – in particular the highly prized nutmeg and clove – would grow only in the Moluccas (depicted here on a map from 1646). At the same time, the Dutch East India Company destroyed all spice production that was not directly under its control, reinforcing the belief that the Moluccas were blessed.

Nearly two centuries would pass before it was discovered that the plants could in fact be cultivated outside this environment. Finally, in 1770, a French **naturalist** managed to smuggle nutmeg and clove seedlings out of the Moluccas and successfully replanted them in Mauritius. With the myth dispelled, the Moluccas spice trade rapidly declined.

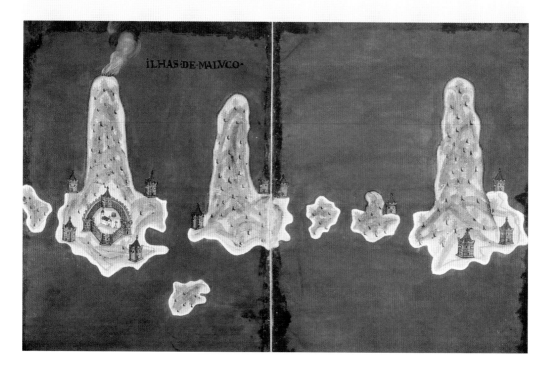

there directly, in order to break the Venetian stranglehold on the trade. The Spice Islands – or East Indies, as the Moluccas were usually known in Europe – were where Christopher Columbus was headed in 1492 when he found his path blocked by America. They were also the destination of the many Portuguese explorers in the early 16th century who sailed down the coast of Africa and then struck out across the Indian Ocean.

The arrival of the Portuguese

In 1511, a Portuguese expedition led by Alfonso d'Albuquerque captured the Muslim port of Malacca on the Malay peninsula. The following year, Portuguese ships dropped anchor in the Banda Islands in the Moluccas. The inhabitants of the Bandas cultivated the nutmeg tree – the source of both nutmeg and mace. From this promising beginning, the Portuguese quickly spread themselves around the Moluccas. For the best part of a century, they enjoyed a near-**monopoly** on the spice trade as it was so much cheaper to transport the cargo by ship than to trek for thousands of kilometres across Asia and eastern Europe.

The Portuguese seemed content with all the money they were making out of the spice trade, and while they built a number of forts, they had little impact on life in Indonesia. During this time, the Muslim **sultanates** continued to expand their influence at the expense of the older Hindu and Buddhist kingdoms.

Then, in 1580, Portugal was annexed by its neighbour and maritime rival, Spain. Spain also possessed the Netherlands, and it was from this new European commercial and sea power that serious foreign intrusion into Indonesia now came. The Dutch first appeared in 1595, when an expedition led by Cornelius de Houtman arrived in Java. Although he returned with a huge cargo of spices, fewer than 100 of the crew of 250 made it back to the Netherlands.

The Dutch East India Company

Portuguese influence over the spice trade was waning, and the Dutch moved quickly to exploit this opening. Several expeditions followed that of Houtman, and by the early years of the 17th century, Dutch merchants had virtually the whole trade to themselves.

There was always the fear, however, that the British would try to muscle in on this lucrative trade. So in 1602, the Dutch government set up the Dutch East

The Dutch East India Company, which ruled in Indonesia from 1602 to 1799, was established to control an entire branch of international trade. This was a new departure in European history.

This painting from 1800 depicts the harbour at Batavia (now Jakarta), the capital of the Dutch East Indies.

India Company and granted it a monopoly on trade in the region. The Dutch East India Company quickly established forts and trading factories at key locations. Company employees, recruited from many different nations, began to function more and more like colonial administrators. Certainly, the company was seen by the Dutch government as an important feature of national policy and a valuable defence against British or other rival trading nations.

The expansion of Dutch rule

Right from the beginning, the Dutch ruled by force. In 1603, Jan Pieterszoon Coen led an invasion force that occupied the Banda Islands, killing many residents in the process. Coen then proceeded to destroy much of the nutmeg and clove production in order to force up the price in European markets. He then turned his attention to Java, where he decided to establish the company's headquarters at Jayakerta (present-day Jakarta).

In 1610, the Dutch were given permission by the local sultan to build a trading station in Jayakerta. When it became apparent that the Dutch were actually erecting a fort, relations between the Jayakerta rulers and the Dutch soured. Although the rulers got help from English adventurers – who were always looking to make mischief for the Dutch – they were defeated by Coen in 1619 and their beloved city was razed.

Coen then built a new city on the spot and named it Batavia. This was the name by which Indonesia's principal city was known until the Japanese occupation of the country, which started in 1942.

Raffles of Singapore

Sir (Thomas) Stamford Raffles (1781–1826), who would later found modern Singapore, was fascinated by Java. He made a survey of the island's many cultural monuments, most notably the temples at Borobudur and Prambanan. He also made studies of Java's wildlife and plants, paid for out of his own pocket. Raffles assembled an impressive zoological collection and, according to his widow's memoirs, kept a host of pets, including a sun bear cub he reared by hand. The little bear often joined the family for dinner, eating mangoes and drinking champagne.

While Raffles was transporting his specimens to England in 1824, a fire onboard ship destroyed much of the unique collection. Nevertheless, he went on to found the Zoological Society of London, to which he submitted papers describing 34 species of birds and thirteen mammals, most of them observed in Sumatra.

Raffles died on the eve of his 45th birthday, but his legacy was to provide a much romanticized model for the administration of the British Empire during succeeding generations.

The Dutch East Indies Company reached the peak of its power around the end of the 17th century, when it boasted 22 factories and had more than 10,000 company employees to manage its far-flung trading interests. These now extended far beyond Indonesia to include Japan, Sri Lanka and South Africa.

During the 18th century, however, the company's fortunes declined as the Netherlands shrunk as a European power. During the 1780s, the Dutch suffered a defeat at the hands of the British and were forced to surrender the Dutch East India Company's monopoly of the spice trade. Revelations of gross mismanagement and **corruption** within the company came to light, and it was disbanded in 1799. All the company's territories passed into the hands of the Dutch government, which meant that most of the Indonesian archipelago became formally part of the Dutch colonial empire.

THE COLONIAL ERA

With Europe occupied by the Napoleonic Wars, the British felt free to scoop up Dutch colonial possessions. In August 1811, a British fleet landed unopposed at Batavia, and Sir Thomas Stamford Raffles (see box on page 61) took control of administering the Dutch East Indies. However, as part of the peace settlement that finally ended the Napoleonic Wars, Britain agreed to hand the colonies back to the Dutch. By 1816, the Dutch East Indies were once more under Dutch rule.

The Dutch were soon caught up in two serious uprisings in Java and Sumatra. In Java, Prince Diponegoro of Yogyakarta was angry that the Dutch were trying to pass over his claims to the sultanate in favour of his younger brother. In 1825, Diponegoro launched a holy war against the Dutch. The prince was supported by all classes of Javanese, from aristocrats to peasants, and it took five years for the Dutch to prevail. An estimated 200,000 Javanese died in the conflict, most of starvation, along with 8000 Dutch soldiers.

Chinese immigrants, who were favoured in commerce by the Dutch overlords, were also a target of the Javanese in the Java War.

Prince Diponegoro – resistance hero

Prince Diponegoro of Yogyakarta had two reasons for his uprising against the Dutch. He felt personal injustice over being denied the inheritance of his father's sultanate. At the same time, his religious nature rebelled at the idea of Dutch infidels (non-Muslims) asserting their authority in Java. The immediate cause of war was the Dutch decision to build a road across a section of Diponegoro's land that contained a sacred tomb – both personal slight and religious insult.

Once war began, Diponegoro's strategy was to wear the Dutch out with hit-and-run attacks, combined with a **scorched-earth policy** intended to leave the enemy without supplies. The strategy came very close to success because the Dutch were ill equipped, both tactically and temperamentally, for this sort of guerrilla war that raged all over central Java. Eventually, however, famine threatened Yogyakarta with ruin, and Diponegoro agreed to peace negotiations. As soon as he put himself in Dutch hands, however, he was arrested and exiled to Sulawesi. He was imprisoned there until his death 25 years later.

Prince Diponegoro is honoured in Indonesia as an early symbol of nationalist sentiment, and his name is on street signs everywhere. His grave in Makassar in Sulawesi is a national monument, and the university at Semarang in the province of Central Java is named after him.

Throughout the Java War, the Dutch had to cope with an unrelated uprising in Sumatra. Fundamentalist Muslims, who had visited Mecca in the early 19th century, were trying to impose a purified form of **Islam** in Sumatra. By 1821, the **zealots**, who called themselves Padri, had succeeded in imposing their beliefs widely throughout central and western Sumatra, even among the fierce Batak tribes. To resist the Padri was to invite death, and the old Sumatran nobility, which found itself targeted, appealed to the Dutch for help. So the Dutch were dragged into a quarrel that really had nothing to do with them. The bitter Padri War dragged on until 1837, and by the time the Dutch finally defeated the Padri, the financial drain of this and the Java War meant that the Dutch East Indies were deeply in debt.

Indigo plants were used to make blue dye – the word 'indigo' also means a type of blue. Today, the blue dye is made synthetically.

The cultivation system

To solve the financial crisis, the Dutch began to employ the so-called cultivation system in Java. This was an agricultural scheme that required villages to set aside one-fifth of their land for the production of export **cash crops**. These crops were to be delivered to the government in place of tax, and then exported to Europe where they were sold on for vast profits.

From the government's point of view, the cultivation system was a spectacular success. Javanese coffee, sugar and indigo (see panel left) were soon pouring into Europe. The value of exports from the Dutch East Indies increased almost sixfold from 1830 to 1840. Huge building projects were financed from the proceeds, including a national railway. Over a 40-year period, nearly one-third of all government revenue in the Netherlands was provided by the cultivation system.

Not surprisingly, it was not such a rosy picture for poor Javanese farmers. The loss of land for rice growing and the burden of spending time and effort to grow the export crops ruined many farmers, particularly those who were impoverished to begin with.

The liberal policy

Under a critical eye, the cultivation system looked uncomfortably similar to **feudalism** (a medieval system in which serfs worked the land for their masters). In the 1860s, it came under attack both on **humanitarian** and economic grounds. It was not abolished outright, but a liberal Dutch government gave up its monopolies over the spice trade and began to phase out its role in sugar cultivation. At the same time, the government started to encourage foreign investment, allowing foreigners to lease land either from Indonesian landowners or, in the case of unoccupied land, from the government, for up to 75 years. This so-called liberal policy did ease the burden on Javanese farmers, although compulsory coffee cultivation was not ended until 1917.

The Indonesian economy really took off under the liberal policy as Dutch investors sank more and more money into their overseas possessions. Exports of coffee, sugar, tea and tobacco soared, and were joined by important new industrial raw materials such as rubber and oil. These developments were accompanied by a big shift in the system of production. Large estates owned by companies began to replace individual small-holdings in Java and particularly along the east coast of Sumatra. In Sumatra, the well-watered lowlands proved ideal for plantation agriculture.

At the same time as the economy was being over-hauled, the Dutch were strengthening their grip on the Indonesian archipelago. Despite having been on the scene for such a long time, by the late 19th century, their presence was patchy and their control was shaky.

Mount Pangrango can be seen in the background in this 1882 illustration of the Botanical Gardens in Jakarta.

Java was quite secure and so were parts of Sumatra, but elsewhere, the Dutch had only a working understanding with local rulers rather than direct colonial administration. All this began to change.

The Dutch tighten their grip

After 35 years, a war with the rulers of Aceh in northern Sumatra finally ended in 1908, bringing the whole island under Dutch control. Bali, Lombok and the island stepping stones towards New Guinea were brought into line, and a presence was established in western New Guinea. In the north, in Sulawesi and the Moluccas (Maluku), long-standing loose arrangements were formalized to spell out Dutch authority, which was also extended from the south coast into central Borneo.

By the early 20th century, therefore, the Dutch East Indies had been effectively brought together as a colonial dependency. The colony required a whole army of

The Chinese quarter in Batavia (now Jakarta) was captured in this illustration dating from 1881. Jakarta today has a large Chinatown.

The ethical policy

When Dutch politician C. T. van Deventer put forward his idea of a 'debt of honour' to the colonies, it struck a chord with an increasingly forward-thinking Dutch society. To some, the ethical policy seemed both right and practical. Money from the central treasury should be used to modernize Indonesian society, bringing Western educational and health standards to everyone. With a healthy, well-educated native population, further prosperity would naturally follow. In time, this could lead to the granting of a large measure of self-rule, in the same way that Canada and Australia had become self-governing British dominions within the British empire.

The ethical policy had to settle for more modest gains. The improved irrigation techniques that were introduced did nothing to bridge the gulf between subsistence rice-growers and plantation owners. More primary and secondary schools were built, however progress was slow, and the literacy rate in colonial days was below 10%.

Although the ethical policy had mixed results, in one entirely unforeseen respect, it had a far-reaching effect. While general educational standards were low, the ethical policy enabled a small, educated elite to develop, from the ranks of which came the first stirrings of an Indonesian nationalist movement.

civil servants to administer the different government departments and services, and clerks were needed to staff the trading businesses.

The ethical policy

The new century brought new ideas about colonial rule, and these would have far-reaching effects. It was plain to see that three decades of the liberal policy had brought prosperity to the colony. It was equally plain, though, that the fruits of the prosperity had not been fairly shared out. A **caste** system based on race had developed, with Europeans living in enclaves in the big cities surrounded by a swelling mass of urban poor. In the countryside, the plantation system enriched European owners, not those who toiled in the fields.

In 1899, an idealistic Dutch politician, C. T. van Deventer, put forward the argument that the colonial rulers, having enriched themselves from the Indies, had a 'debt of honour' to put something back (see box on page 67). This debt should take the form of improving education and health, and introducing agricultural practices that would stimulate the growth of the rural village economy. This was called the **ethical** policy, which was started in 1901 to achieve these ends.

THE RISE OF NATIONALISM

Twentieth-century **nationalism** in Indonesia ran a similar course to nationalism elsewhere in Asia and Africa. A mainly young, educated **elite** grew up who, because of their education, felt Westernized but alienated from the dominant Dutch colonialist society. Nationalists resented specific injustices – such as economic and social discrimination. At the same time, they were interested in questions of Indonesian cultural identity, and sometimes in internationalist movements such as **socialism** and **communism**. This unrest led to the formation of new political movements and parties.

The leaders of the Indonesian Communist Party (PKI) are pictured here in 1925. The party formed in the 1920s but played little part in the country's struggle for independence.

Nationalist political parties

In 1912, the Indies Party was founded by the Eurasian E. F. E. Douwes Dekker, who felt that Eurasians were unfairly discriminated against by the Dutch. The party's slogan was 'The Indies for those who live there'. That same year saw the emergence of the Islamic Association, which, under its dynamic chairman Omar Said Tjokroaminto, quickly gained a mass following. By 1919, it claimed a membership of 2.5 million. While this was certainly a gross overestimate, the Islamic Association was by far the largest of the nationalist movements. Then, in 1914, the Dutchman Hendricus Sneevliet founded the Indies Social Democratic Association. This became a communist party in the early 1920s and changed its name to the Indonesian Communist Party (Partai Kommunist Indonesia, or PKI).

In the long run, the PKI was to play little part in the struggle for Indonesian nationhood. It launched uprisings in Java in 1926 and in western Sumatra in 1927. When these were crushed by the Dutch authorities, the PKI faded away – at least for the time being.

With the Islamic Association also in decline, the way was open for a new, broad-based nationalist movement. It came in 1927 with the formation of the Indonesian Nationalist Party (Partai Nasional Indonesia, PNI), which was led by a young graduate engineer, Achmed Sukarno. The PNI claimed that the task facing nationalists was to overthrow Dutch rule, and that arguments about what should take its place were a distraction from that overriding priority.

Throughout the 1930s, nationalist parties grouped and regrouped as the Dutch authorities tried to keep them in check by arresting their leaders. Sukarno spent periods in prison, as well as a long time in exile from Java. So, too, did another charismatic nationalist leader, Muhammad Hatta, who, with Sukarno, rose to become a leading figure in the movement. By the beginning of World War Two in 1939, however, there were fears

Starting with the Padri War (1821–37) and the Java War (1825–30), Islam became the symbol of opposition to the Dutch in Indonesia. A century later, Islamic parties were the main players in the rise of nationalism.

about the threat posed to the independence of the Netherlands by Nazi Germany. Such fears meant that political agitation for Indonesian independence was put on hold. That was the way matters stood when, at the beginning of 1942, the victorious Japanese came storming on to the scene.

The Japanese occupation

Following their surprise attack on the US fleet at Pearl Harbor on 7 December 1941, the Japanese rapidly overran all of Southeast Asia, including the Dutch East Indies. Initially, they were looked upon as liberators, as they interned 175,000 Dutch residents and promised to work with Indonesian nationalists.

Wherever they went during World War Two, the Japanese preached the doctrine of the 'Greater East Asia co-prosperity sphere'. This appeared to be anticolonial, with its implied promise of Asia for the Asians. However, before long, it became apparent that what the Japanese really had in mind was Asia for the Japanese. It also became clear that their eyes were firmly fixed on the plentiful oil and rubber that Indonesia could provide for their war machine, not on independence for the Indonesian people.

Towards the end of the war, however, staring defeat in the face, the Japanese concluded that anything was better than the triumphant return of European imperialists to their corner of the world. Just before the **atom bombs** fell on Hiroshima and Nagasaki in August 1945, the Japanese invited Sukarno and Hatta to Saigon, Vietnam, and offered them the opportunity to take over control in their own country.

THE STRUGGLE FOR INDEPENDENCE

On 17 August, after receiving news of Japan's unconditional surrender to the USA, Sukarno proclaimed the Republic of Indonesia. But proclaiming independence was not the same thing as achieving it. Immediately, the

Although the Japanese quickly earned a reputation for being harsh rulers during their occupation of Indonesia, they did allow Indonesians to have more responsibility in government than the Dutch had ever allowed.

The Japanese forces march into Kendari in Sulawesi in January 1942. They were to occupy Indonesia for the next three years.

new republic was confronted by thousands of British troops. They arrived in Indonesia to supervise the surrender of the Japanese forces and to reimpose Dutch rule. The British found themselves caught between their Dutch allies, who were determined to reclaim their colony, and the new Indonesian authorities, who were determined to prevent that happening. There were

The battle for Surabaya

In accordance with Japan's policy at the end of World War Two, when they faced certain defeat, the Japanese commander in the Surabaya region ordered his men to surrender their arms to the Indonesian nationalists, not to the Dutch who were trying to re-establish their authority. This prompted the British, towards the end of October 1945, to land 6000 troops from the British Indian Army at Surabaya. The troops were to evacuate Dutch refugees, who had been released from internment in Japanese camps and now found themselves in a dangerous position.

To the distress of the British, their 6000 soldiers were confronted by over 100,000 Indonesian nationalists – some of whom were members of the newly formed People's Security Army but most of whom were armed civilians.

In an attempt to calm the situation, the British flew in Sukarno and Hatta, who tried but failed to arrange a ceasefire. When the British commander was killed, the British brought in reinforcements and attacked Surabaya using air power and well-equipped, experienced ground forces.

The Indonesians put up fierce resistance, but after three weeks, the city fell to the British. The date of the British assault, 10 November, is commemorated as Hero's Day, and the battle is credited with inspiring Indonesians with the belief that they could stand up to European imperialists.

many bloody incidents, including a savage battle for Surabaya, the second city of Java (see box above).

In 1946, the British left Indonesia, relieved to let the Dutch take over the handling of their own messy colonial legacy. For the next two years, the situation was very confusing, as the Dutch switched back and forth between diplomacy and force in an attempt to resolve the conflict between their own, colonial aims and those of the nationalists.

By 1948, however, the United Nations (UN) – led by the USA, which believed **colonialism** to be a relic of the past – opposed the continued Dutch occupation of Indonesia. In August 1949, the Netherlands agreed to pull out, retaining only what is now Papua. On 27 December 1949, Indonesia gained independence, which was finally recognized by the world.

THE SUKARNO YEARS

The first decade of Indonesian independence was a time of political turmoil. Muslims, communists and various regional and minority interests were all jostling for position within the parliamentary system established by the Constitution. Governments came and went with bewildering speed, until, in the late 1950s, President Sukarno began arguing that Western-style **democracy** was unsuited to the country's circumstances.

Instead, he put forward his own vision of what he called 'guided democracy' (see box on page 74) as the only way of resolving the political crisis. In July 1959, with anarchy threatening to overwhelm the nation, Sukarno was able to push through a new Constitution by presidential decree. The new Constitution put the president at the head of the government, whereas before he was simply head of state. 'Guided democracy' was now the watchword.

British soldiers search Indonesian men in Jakarta in December 1945. The British had arrived after World War Two to help the Dutch reassert their authority in the colony.

Guided democracy

What Sukarno meant by 'guided democracy' was a return to the way in which Indonesian villages had traditionally arrived at decisions. Instead of majority rule, with winners and losers, village democracy meant that everyone had their say, and then a consensus would be reached that everyone could agree to. In practice, respected village elders played a crucial role in resolving conflicting views. In applying guided democracy, Sukarno took over the role of village elder himself, deciding on what the consensus should be after listening to all the arguments. This led to the charge that Sukarno was really trying to establish a dictatorship, disguised under the slogan of 'guided democracy'.

During the first half of the 1960s, Sukarno was a major figure in the world. He saw himself as a leader of what were then called the non-aligned nations, steering Indonesia between the shores of Western capitalism and the communism of the then Soviet Union. What this meant in practice was that Sukarno took an aggressive stance against the old imperialist powers on his borders.

Having already seized assets owned by Dutch and British companies in Indonesia, Sukarno launched a campaign to force the Dutch to surrender their last possession in the archipelago, Netherlands New Guinea (now Papua). This aggressive policy was called *konfrontasi* (confrontation), and in 1963, the Dutch capitulated and handed over their colony to the UN. It became the Indonesian province of Irian Jaya in 1969.

Next, Sukarno turned his attention to the new Federation of Malaysia. The federation included two provinces on the island of Borneo, and it, too, came in for a bruising encounter with *konfrontasi*. Along the frontier with Kalimantan (the Indonesian part of Borneo), Indonesian forces and Malaysian and British **counter-insurgency** forces waged a jungle campaign.

The policy of *konfrontasi* increasingly drew Sukarno's Indonesia into the former Soviet Union's sphere of influence. The Soviet Union was a willing provider of arms for Sukarno's campaigns against 'Western imperialists'. It also provided financial support when Indonesia's economy started to falter under the burden of *konfrontasi* and Sukarno's grand building schemes. Growing dependence on the Soviet Union and, increasingly, communist China greatly increased the influence of the Indonesian Communist Party (PKI). The party, along with the army and Sukarno's personal charisma, became a vital guarantor of Sukarno's authority.

The slaughter of the communists

The uneasy alliance between the PKI and the army fell apart in October 1965, when a group of left-wing officers attempted to stage a *coup d'état*. In the course of a confusing night, they murdered six senior generals, and chaos engulfed Indonesia.

The coup attempt itself was quickly snuffed out by quick action on the part of General Suharto, a 45-year-old veteran of the independence struggle. The aftermath,

Robert F. Kennedy – the then US attorney-general – is pictured here in discussion with President Sukarno in 1964 during the Malaysian crisis.

Hundreds of thousands of people who were alleged to be communists were killed after the failed coup. Some estimates put the figure at 500,000, while others run to a million.

however, was horrific. The PKI and its communist Chinese backers were blamed for the coup attempt, but this charge remains a matter of historical as well as political dispute. Nevertheless, there was an overwhelming backlash against the PKI and anyone suspected of supporting it, and against the Chinese in Indonesia. The army turned a blind eye as anticommunist riots in Jakarta spread into the Java countryside and then throughout Indonesia. Entire villages in east and central Java and Bali were annihilated. Streets ran red with blood and rivers were choked with corpses.

Throughout this bloody turmoil, Suharto slowly but steadily elbowed Sukarno aside as he consolidated the army's control of the government. In 1967, Sukarno was finally stripped of all power, and the following year, Suharto became president.

SUHARTO'S NEW ORDER

The Suharto take-over represented a decisive break with Indonesia's past – the replacement of what was called the Old Order with the New Order. For the next three decades, there was political stability in Indonesia and, at the start, a nearly miraculous economic recovery.

Suharto quickly wound down the policy of *konfrontasi*, and repositioned Indonesia as a friend of the West in order to attract overseas investment. The Indonesian economy grew rapidly in the 1970s, thanks mainly to expanding oil, gas and timber exports. Then in the 1980s and 1990s, as foreign investment came pouring in, manufacturing for export further strengthened the economy, stabilizing the currency and reducing the traditional reliance on exporting raw materials.

The political stability and prosperity that came with the New Order, however, came with a price. While Suharto was careful to avoid the creation of a military regime, his government was clearly underpinned from the beginning by military power. Suharto won a long sequence of five-year presidential terms from 1968 to the mid-1990s. Not only was opposition stifled, but power was concentrated in the hands of a small group of Suharto loyalists, including family members. This situation inevitably sowed the seeds of corruption, which would eventually discredit the regime.

The end of the Suharto regime

In 1975, Indonesia became involved in a conflict in East Timor, which led to many years of brutal occupation and repression (see box on page 78). It was another drain on the nation's overstretched resources, and by the 1990s, the so-called economic miracle of the New Order was unravelling. Wealth had never been distributed widely, which meant that a fairly small rich class lived sheltered from the surrounding poverty. It became apparent to outside observers and some Indonesians that the Suharto regime was financially corrupt as well as politically repressive. In particular, it was alleged that the president and his family had amassed personal fortunes amounting to many billions of pounds.

General Suharto pictured in 1966, a year after the failed coup. He is addressing the special military tribunal that would try the former deputy premier, Subandrio, for his alleged involvement with the coup.

The bloody birth of East Timor

While all the rest of Indonesia was a Dutch colonial possession, Timor was divided between the Dutch in the west and the Portuguese in the east. When the Portuguese left in 1975, East Timor rapidly descended into civil war as various factions struggled for control. Some wanted to join Indonesia, while others desired independence.

Suharto's Indonesian army settled the matter in December 1975 by occupying East Timor and incorporating it into the Republic of Indonesia the following year. The United Nations (UN) condemned the annexation of East Timor. The resistance movement there feared being occupied by a brutal regime bent on economic development and political repression of any opposition. Suharto's attempts to crush the resistance became an international byword for **atrocity**.

As Indonesia was generally successful in hiding its activities in East Timor, the true extent of the horror that the contested province suffered remains unknown. However, it is thought that at least 100,000 people and maybe double that number – out of a population of only 750,000 – were killed or died from the effects of Indonesia's 'pacification' programme.

A growing international protest over human rights abuses in East Timor accompanied the final stages of Suharto's rule. When he fell from power in 1998, it seemed that progress was possible. In August 1999, a referendum in East Timor showed a clear majority in favour of independence. But both during and after the referendum campaign, the bloodshed continued as pro-Indonesian **militias** ran a 'scorched-earth' campaign, causing thousands to flee their homes. Indonesian President Habibie asked for a UN peace-keeping force to be sent in to administer the troubled region, and in October 1999, the UN agreed with his request.

In May 2002, East Timor finally gained its independence, and by 2003, the UN presence was much reduced.

In late 1997, Asia was plunged into financial crisis, throwing Indonesia into turmoil. It paralysed the economy and provoked a currency collapse, with the rupiah losing 80 per cent of its value against the US dollar. A stock market crash followed. The International Monetary Fund (IMF) came to Indonesia's rescue with a £27,000 million rescue package, but the IMF's terms included removing members of Suharto's family and his corrupt cronies from well-paid positions.

When Suharto proved unwilling or unable to meet the IMF's demands, foreign investors began pulling out of the country, the rupiah went into free fall and student demonstrators took to the streets.

In the end, Suharto bowed to international pressure and stepped down. He was replaced by his vice-president, B. J. Habibie, but Habibie was too tainted by the Suharto regime and did not survive. In 1999, in a closely contested election, Sukarno's daughter, Megawati Sukarnoputri, won the greatest support but was deprived of the presidency by an alliance of Muslim parties opposed to a woman president. She agreed to serve as vice-president under the new president, Abdurrahman Wahid, a Muslim cleric, but Wahid lost his support in parliament and was removed in July 2001. Sukarnoputri then assumed the presidency. Her father is still widely revered as the nation's founding father, and there is hope in Indonesia and abroad that Sukarnoputri's presidency will bring a period of stability.

Indonesians flock to the polls during the general elections in February 1998. President Suharto was re-elected but would be forced to step down just three months later after massive riots that claimed hundreds of lives.

INDONESIA'S GOVERNMENT

The Constitution of the Republic of Indonesia is generally referred to as the 1945 Constitution. That was the year it was first drafted and adopted by Indonesian nationalists. It is the Constitution that President Sukarno imposed in place of a federal system in 1959. It has great significance for Indonesians because it expresses the ideals and goals of independence, and because it was inspired by philosophical principles that underlie the Indonesian approach to life.

These principles are summed up in the word 'Pancasila' (pronounced *pan-cha-see-la*), which means 'five principles'. The five principles are: belief in the one and only God (this can mean any god, not just the Muslim Allah); a just and civilized humanity; the unity of Indonesia; guided democracy (see page 74) arising from representative government; and peace and social justice.

The president of Indonesia is both head of state and head of government. The president and vice-president are elected for a five-year term by an electoral college called the People's Consultative Assembly, which also approves the broad outlines of national policy. The assembly is comprised of 700 members, 500 of whom

Most members of the House of Representatives are democratically elected. The People's Consultative Assembly meets only every five years following an election to elect the president and vice-president and to approve national policy.

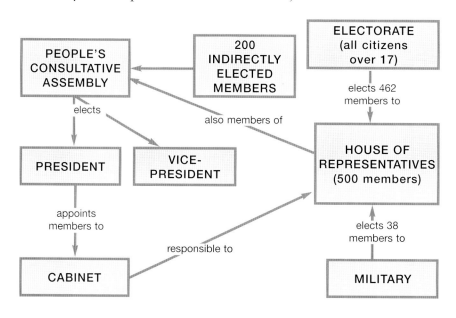

80

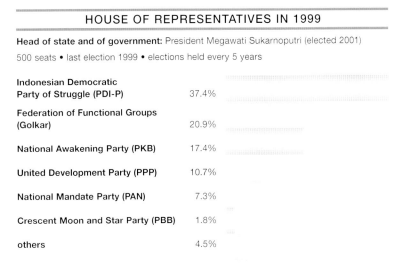

HOUSE OF REPRESENTATIVES IN 1999

Head of state and of government: President Megawati Sukarnoputri (elected 2001)

500 seats • last election 1999 • elections held every 5 years

Indonesian Democratic Party of Struggle (PDI-P)	37.4%
Federation of Functional Groups (Golkar)	20.9%
National Awakening Party (PKB)	17.4%
United Development Party (PPP)	10.7%
National Mandate Party (PAN)	7.3%
Crescent Moon and Star Party (PBB)	1.8%
others	4.5%

The elections in 1999 were the first democratic elections held in Indonesia for more than 30 years. Members of the House of Representatives serve five-year terms.

are the members of the parliament, the House of Representatives. Of the parliament's 500 members, 462 are directly elected by popular vote and 38 are appointed as representatives of the military. The balance of seats in the People's Consultative Assembly is made up of 200 indirectly elected members.

The 1999 elections

During the Suharto years, no real political opposition was tolerated, but after he fell from power in 1998, dozens of political parties sprang up and have continued to form and reform ever since. In the election of June 1999, the first democratic election in over 30 years, five parties emerged with significant support.

Sukarnoputri's Indonesian Democratic Party of Struggle (PDI-P) won the most seats and signalled a rejection of the New Order policies followed by Suharto. The party enjoyed strong working-class and nationalist support. Golkar – the main party when Suharto was in power and which was backed by the New Order – came a close second, and Muslim parties took the next three places. A coalition of these leading parties formed the new government, which, from 2001, was led by President Megawati Sukarnoputri.

The economy

'After the bombing, construction work stopped because the tourists were not coming, so the economy ground to a halt.'

Balinese resident on the economic impact of the Bali bombings in 2002

During the Asian economic crisis, which started in late 1997, the Indonesian economy set off on a very bumpy ride. The rupiah collapsed, and **gross national product (GNP)** fell by 13.7 per cent in 1998 – a very bad performance that reflected investors' lack of confidence and the fact that massive amounts of money were leaving the country. Foreign investment fell by nearly two-thirds between 1997 and 1999. The political fall-out from the economic crisis forced President Suharto from office after more than 30 years in power, and led to the first free elections for decades in 1999.

The economy began to stabilize in 1999 and showed signs of growth by the beginning of the 21st century. However, it remains in a precarious position and is heavily dependent on help from the International Monetary Fund (IMF). The IMF has insisted on a series of economic reforms, and it is only by putting these

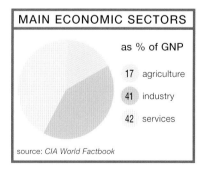

MAIN ECONOMIC SECTORS

as % of GNP

17   agriculture
41   industry
42   services

source: *CIA World Factbook*

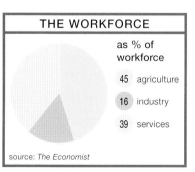

THE WORKFORCE

as % of workforce

45   agriculture
16   industry
39   services

source: *The Economist*

Bamboo is being transported as rafts on a river in Sulawesi. Rice, cotton, coffee and sugar cane are also important crops on the island.

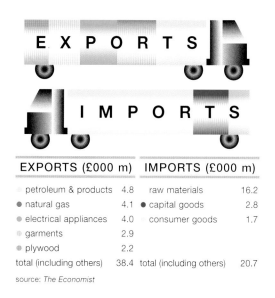

EXPORTS (£000 m)		IMPORTS (£000 m)	
petroleum & products	4.8	raw materials	16.2
natural gas	4.1	capital goods	2.8
electrical appliances	4.0	consumer goods	1.7
garments	2.9		
plywood	2.2		
total (including others)	38.4	total (including others)	20.7

source: *The Economist*

reforms into practice that Indonesia can continue to expect international financial support.

All this is in stark contrast to the 1980s and early 1990s, when economic growth rates averaged nearly 5 per cent, rising to 8 per cent in 1996, just before the Asian economic crisis. In that year, with no signs of the crisis that would occur, a report by the World Bank praised Indonesia's economic performance, describing it as one of the very best in the world.

NATURAL RESOURCES

A copper mine in Papua. Indonesia is the third-largest producer of copper in the world.

Indonesia is one of the wealthiest countries in the world in terms of natural resources, and the long period of growth was created and largely sustained by exploiting these enormous natural resources. Chief among the

HOW INDONESIA USES ITS LAND

crop land

forest

pasture

wetland

country's natural resources – and Indonesia's major source of export revenue – are large reserves of oil and natural gas. Most of the country's oil and gas deposits are in Sumatra. Indonesian oil fields pump about 1.5 million barrels of crude oil per day, and the country ranks 16th in world oil production. Indonesia is the only Asian member of the Organization of Petroleum-Exporting Countries (OPEC).

In addition to oil and natural gas, Indonesia has great wealth in its rainforests, which account for around half of the world's trade in tropical hardwoods. There is also abundant palm, rattan and bamboo. However, international environmental groups are greatly concerned about the deforestation of Indonesia's precious hardwoods. Along with the great Amazonian rainforest of South America, the tropical forests of Indonesia are considered to be of critical importance to the planet as a whole. The pressure on the rainforest comes from two sources – population growth and the profit that can be made from timber-related industries.

Indonesia is rich in mineral resources. The main minerals that are mined are tin, bauxite and silver, but nickel, copper, manganese and gold are also significant. In 1993, Indonesia's coal industry was opened up to foreign investment, which has resulted in major joint

Large parts of Indonesia are covered in tropical forest, although much of Java is given over to growing crops. There are significant wetland areas on the east coast of Sumatra, in southern Kalimantan and in Papua.

ENERGY SOURCES

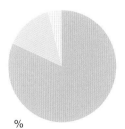

%

87 oil, gas, coal & diesel

10 hydroelectricity

3 other

source: *CIA World Factbook*

Deforestation and illegal logging

Along with Brazil and the Congo, Indonesia has the most biologically diverse and important forests in the world – at least for the time being. As recently as the beginning of the 20th century, forest accounted for nearly 85% of the total land area of the 18,000 or so islands. In fact, deforestation did not occur on a significant level until the early 1970s, when timber-related industries formed part of the export drive under President Suharto's New Order (see page 76).

The pulp and paper industry has been the chief agent of deforestation, having increased its capacity by 700% during the 1990s and the early years of the 21st century. An annual deforestation rate of a little over 1.5 million hectares (3.5 million acres) is having a devastating environmental effect.

Lowland tropical forests have taken the brunt of the onslaught, and it is feared that on present trends they will be wiped out on Sumatra by 2005. The loss of these forests brings with it the destruction of habitat for a diverse range of wildlife and plants. The orangutan is just one of the animals in danger (see pages 24–5). There is also the related environmental disaster of an increase in carbon emissions and global warming that the loss of rainforest leads to.

In a country such as Indonesia, it is perfectly possible to have a sustainable timber industry – that is, one where the forests have time to grow back – but it would mean putting limits on logging. Under the Suharto regime, there were no such limits, and hardwood species such as the highly prized ramin were ruthlessly exploited. Rampant illegal logging was tolerated and even encouraged, as wealthy timber barons took their place among the Suharto inner circle of family and friends busily plundering the country.

With the fall of Suharto, there came the prospect of change. In 2000, the government imposed a ban on further destruction of virgin rainforest. The following year, at Indonesia's request, ramin was placed on the endangered list and all trade in it made illegal. These are encouraging signs, but illegal logging has to date proved impossible to stop.

ventures with overseas partners. Coal production reached 92.5 million tonnes in 2001, and more than two-thirds of the total was exported.

In 1998, the value of Indonesian gold production reached £625 million, followed closely by the value of copper production. Also of commercial significance are large salt reserves in shallow coastal lagoons.

It is believed that Indonesia contains substantial quantities of iron and uranium, but these resources have not yet been tapped.

These workers are panning for gold in a mine in Jayapura, Papua. Indonesia ranks eighth in the world for its gold production.

AGRICULTURE

Indonesia, and in particular densely populated Java, is a fertile country. About 10 per cent of the land is arable and a little over 7 per cent is under permanent cultivation. Agriculture contributes 17 per cent of Indonesia's GNP and employs 45

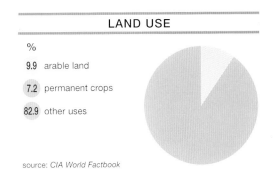

LAND USE

%
9.9 arable land
7.2 permanent crops
82.9 other uses

source: *CIA World Factbook*

A terraced rice field in Java. The rich volcanic soils of Java are ideal for growing rice in flooded rice fields. This method of growing rice has been practised for more than 2000 years, and terraced rice fields are a common sight on both Java and Bali.

per cent of its workforce. Rice is the principal crop, although soya beans, cassava, yams, peanuts and fruit are also widely cultivated.

The self-sufficient peasant farmer tending terraced rice fields is a conspicuous feature of Indonesian life. The country is also the home of widespread plantation agriculture, such as for rubber, and is one of the world's leading rubber producers. The plantation system also lends itself to growing sugar cane, tea, coffee, palm oil, cocoa, sisal, tobacco – and, of course, the famous cloves and nutmeg and other exotic spices that first drew outsiders to Indonesia many centuries ago.

The national smoke

The smell of *kretek* (clove cigarettes) is a distinctive feature of Indonesian street life. Mixing tobacco with cloves is a centuries-old practice in Java, and it is big business today. Over 90 per cent of cigarettes smoked in

Indonesia are a mixture (40 per cent cloves, 60 per cent tobacco is the favoured blend). The *kretek* industry employs 4 million people, and only oil revenues contribute more taxes.

THE DRIVE FOR INDUSTRIALIZATION
Indonesia's export economy was given a tremendous boost when the Arab–Israeli Yom Kippur War in 1973 resulted in a quadrupling of oil prices. The government owned all oil and mineral rights, so money poured into

Sumatra and Java are the most industrialized islands, and timber processing is important throughout Indonesia.

MAJOR INDUSTRIES

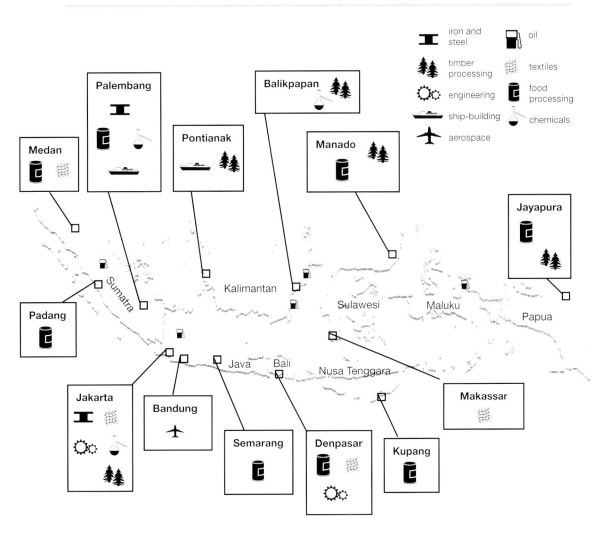

iron and steel — oil

timber processing — textiles

engineering — food processing

ship-building — chemicals

aerospace

Palembang

Balikpapan

Medan

Pontianak

Manado

Jayapura

Padang

Sumatra

Kalimantan

Sulawesi

Maluku

Papua

Java

Bali

Nusa Tenggara

Jakarta

Bandung

Makassar

Semarang

Denpasar

Kupang

the treasury. While much of this was siphoned off as bribes and other forms of **corruption**, some, at least, was used to build roads and schools and to improve methods of rice production.

When oil prices went down in the early 1980s, the Suharto regime channelled resources into the manufacturing sector in order to boost export earnings. From that time, non-oil exports steadily increased, and by the mid-1990s, manufacturing accounted for 20 per cent of Indonesia's GNP. The industrial sector includes: textile, clothing and shoe manufacture, electronics, chemicals, rubber tyres and cement. By 2001, industry (including oil) accounted for 41 per cent of Indonesia's GNP, with services contributing 42 per cent.

Much of Indonesia's export success has stemmed from cheap prices, made possible by the pitifully low wages paid to the workforce. Apart from the fact that such sweatshop labour is unethical, it has a history of not promoting economic stability or sustained growth.

Demonstrators in Jakarta in 1965 demand that the government take over foreign oil companies. Resentment of foreign economic influence in Indonesia helped weaken the position of President Sukarno, who was overthrown two years later.

Indonesia's trading partners

With the exception of the USA, Indonesia's largest trading partners are in Asia. Its exports for 2002 were about £34,500 million. Japan took more than 19% of these exports, followed by the USA and Singapore. South Korea, China and Taiwan were also significant markets for Indonesian-made goods.

In the same year, Indonesia's imports totalled £21,200 million. Japan was the main import trading partner, with more than 18%, followed by South Korea and Singapore. Next came China, the USA and Australia. Machinery and equipment, chemicals and fuels make up the bulk of Indonesia's imports.

The collapse in the value of the rupiah in the late 1990s has left Indonesia with an external debt estimated in 2001 at £84,400 million. It was at this time that the International Monetary Fund (IMF) came to the rescue with a £27,000 million loan. Between 1997 and 2002, the rupiah slumped from just under

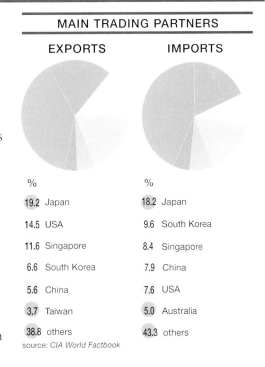

MAIN TRADING PARTNERS

EXPORTS		IMPORTS	
%		%	
19.2	Japan	18.2	Japan
14.5	USA	9.6	South Korea
11.6	Singapore	8.4	Singapore
6.6	South Korea	7.9	China
5.6	China	7.6	USA
3.7	Taiwan	5.0	Australia
38.8	others	43.3	others

source: *CIA World Factbook*

Rp 4800 to the pound to over Rp 16,000. On the one hand, such a dramatic decline benefits exporters because it makes exports cheap on the international market. On the other hand, it makes it very difficult to afford imported goods.

The moment an even cheaper alternative appears somewhere in the world, the market moves on to exploit it, and then moves elsewhere and so on.

The abuse of child labour is commonplace in a country such as Indonesia where children's education depends on where they live and how much money their family has. It is impossible to put an accurate figure on a practice that can so easily be hidden, but some estimates suggest that as many as 10 million Indonesian children are being exploited.

Beautiful batik

Textiles rank just behind oil and natural gas as Indonesia's second-largest industry. Batik is the most famous of Indonesian textiles, with its motifs of flowers, birds, butterflies and geometric patterns. The heart of the batik industry is in Java, but it also flourishes in Madura and, to a lesser extent, in Bali, Lombok and Sulawesi. Batik is exported around the world, and it also accounts for a significant proportion of the money tourists spend in Indonesia.

The craft of batik, which is Javanese for 'wax painting', is hundreds of years old and is particularly associated with the sultan's court at Yogyakarta in central Java. Beeswax or paraffin wax is applied in patterns to fine machine-woven cottons, which are then dyed. Everything not covered in wax takes up the dye. For heavier fabrics, the wax is applied on both sides, which requires great skill to create matching patterns. The traditional dyes are deep blues, reds and browns, although today chemical dyes are used for greater variety and brilliance of colour.

There are two methods of applying the beeswax. In traditional batik, the patterns are drawn on with a *canting*, which is a copper spout attached to a wooden or bamboo handle. The *canting* is dipped into a pot of molten wax, and the wax is allowed to flow on to the cloth from the spout like ink from a pen. Traditional batik is the preserve of women.

In the 19th century, batik manufacture was mechanized to a certain extent to enable the industry to compete with cheap European textiles. The fabric is stretched on to long tables, and a copper stamping tool with the desired pattern is dipped into hot wax and then pressed onto the cloth. The stamping tool, called a *cap*, enables the design to be repeated many times, greatly increasing output. The stamping is generally done by men.

Indonesia has been plagued by labour unrest – not only because of dissatisfaction with poor wages but also because of racial tensions between the ethnic Chinese, who own most of the businesses, and the workers, who are almost all ethnic Malays.

TRANSPORTATION

Indonesia's railway network is confined to the densely populated island of Java and parts of Sumatra. There are few major roads in the remote provinces of Kalimantan and Papua. Bali has an international airport to service its tourist industry, which is of great importance to the island's economy.

——— major roads
++++++ railways
——— major rivers
✈ major airports

Another disturbing feature of the Indonesian economy is the inequality of wealth distribution – both between rich and poor, and between the islands. This inequality is in part a legacy of President Suharto's corrupt regime, and also a reflection of Indonesia's failure to develop a large middle class – the middle class represents only 7 per cent of the population.

Foreign investment and the factories and transport links that are essential to create a modern manufacturing base are concentrated, like the Indonesian population, in Java. In outlying regions such as Papua and Kalimantan, most people struggle along at a subsistence level, as they have always done.

TRANSPORTATION

Because most of the distances between the population centres are usually short, road transport is the most important way of moving passengers and freight. The islands of Java, Sumatra, Bali and Madura have paved highways, but more remote areas such as Maluku and Papua have relatively few roads, the majority of which are unpaved. Because most freight travels by road or by sea, the railway is not economically significant.

The Bali bombings

The beachside town of Kuta was busy with holiday-makers on Saturday night, 12 October 2002. Kuta is the hub of the Bali tourist industry, a hugely popular destination for Australian holiday-makers and for young backpackers the world over. Just before midnight, two car bombs exploded in quick succession, the first outside Paddy's Irish Pub and the second outside the Sari Club. A fireball engulfed the Sari Club, and by the time the flames burnt themselves out, more than 200 people were dead or dying and several hundred more were injured.

Almost half of the victims were young Australians, although holiday-makers from twenty other countries perished too, along with local Balinese people.

Over the following months, 30 people, all of them Indonesian, were arrested and put on trial in connection with the **atrocity**. Three were sentenced to death, one to life imprisonment, and twelve to jail terms ranging from seven to sixteen years.

The bombing is believed to be the work of the Jemaah Islamiyah terrorist group, which is thought to be linked

The beachside town of Kuta on the island of Bali has long been a popular destination for Australian holiday-makers, particularly those who come for Bali's world-famous surf beaches.

Police examine the site of the bombing in the Sari Club the day after the incident. The Bali bombing was the most deadly terrorist attack since September 11th.

with Osama bin Laden's al-Qaeda network. It had the hallmarks of an al-Qaeda operation – a soft target, good organization and a horrific human toll.

Why Bali and why that particular venue? Bali has long enjoyed a reputation as a tolerant and peaceful tourist haven. Because it had escaped the sort of civil violence that has afflicted much of Indonesia, security considerations were far from anyone's mind.

Most Balinese are Hindu, but relations between them and the **Muslim** minority on the island have traditionally been good. Relations have been good, too, between the Balinese and the free-spending tourists who are so important for the island's (and Indonesia's)

prosperity. The Sari Club was typical of the way Bali has accommodated Western tastes to attract the tourist pound. It was an open-air bar and disco, where young Westerners were encouraged to party late into the night. Apart from staff and those accompanying foreigners, locals were not allowed on the premises.

In retrospect, this made the Sari Club a natural target for two reasons. It was bound to be packed with Westerners, which guaranteed high casualty figures and maximum global impact. It also symbolized much of what Islamic fundamentalists detest about Western society and dislike seeing in their midst – an alcohol-fuelled nightclub culture that they consider an affront to decency.

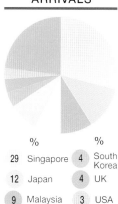

During the late 1990s, the stock market in Jakarta saw shares lose their value overnight.

MAIN FOREIGN ARRIVALS

%		%	
29	Singapore	4	South Korea
12	Japan	4	UK
9	Malaysia	3	USA
8	Taiwan	3	Germany
8	Australia	20	others

source:
Government of Indonesia

The Indonesian State Railway (Perusahaan Jawatan Kereta Api, or PJKA) has 6458 kilometres (4013 miles) of track, mainly on Java, but geography makes rail transport impractical for most islands. The rolling stock is often outdated and in poor condition, which means that rail transport can be unreliable.

As would be expected in a nation of islands, water transport is important. Ferry and cargo services link the islands, and larger vessels ship commodities such as petroleum, rice, coconut oil and wood to East Asia and the rest of the world. The major ports are Tanjungpriok, near Jakarta, Tanjungperak at Surabaya, Belawan near Medan, Batam and Makassar.

There are international airports on Java, Sumatra, Bali, Lombok, Kalimantan and Biak. Services within Indonesia are provided by the state airline, Garuda.

TOURISM

Tourism is Indonesia's third-largest industry after oil and textiles, and in 2001, it contributed 5.4 per cent to the country's GNP. However, the tourist industry was dealt a harsh blow with the Bali nightclub bombing in 2002 (see box on pages 94–5). In 2001, before the attack, around 35 per cent of Indonesia's 5.2 million foreign visitors arrived at the island's international airport. Foreign exchange from tourism fell during the year by around 20 per cent from £3400 million to £2700 million. By early 2003, however, progress made by the Indonesian authorities in convicting the suspected bombers seemed to have improved confidence levels. The tourist trade remained well down on normal, but there were some signs of recovery.

Tourism in Indonesia appears to have arrived at a crossroads. The archipelago contains magnificent scenery and a wealth of wildlife and plants. It also possesses a unique cultural diversity and artistic tresures. On the face of it, Indonesia should be a prime tourist destination. But the tourist industry has been held back by poorly developed transport links and tourist facilities, by poor planning and by a chronic lack of funds. Add to that the security concerns brought to the world's attention by the bombings, and it is clear that Indonesia has a long way to go to be able to capitalize fully on its tourist potential.

The distinctive shape of a Batak house near Lake Toba in Sumatra. With its many cultures, Indonesia is an attractive destination for foreign visitors, but the country still has some way to go to make the most of its tourist industry.

Arts and living

'We are the world's cultural heirs.'

Preface to Angkatan 45, the nationalist literary movement
formed at the end of World War Two

The cultural diversity found in Indonesia is so enormous that it is impossible to talk of 'Indonesian culture', 'Indonesian art and architecture' and so on. However, although the archipelago is made up of many different peoples and cultural groupings, unifying features such as a sense of national identity, help create a picture of Indonesian life.

THE ARTS

Shadow-puppet theatre, Balinese dance and **gamelan** music are probably the most widely recognized of the Indonesian arts. Yet these represent only a small fraction of the astonishing diversity of cultural activity to be found in the archipelago.

Language and literature

Perhaps the most important unifying feature of Indonesian life is Bahasa Indonesia – the Indonesian language, which is in fact a version of Malay that has been given a national name. Considering that there are over 400 languages and **dialects** spoken across the islands, it is a considerable achievement to have settled on one as a national language.

It is also significant that the language agreed on by the young nationalists at the All Indonesia Youth Congress in 1928 (see box on page 101) was Malay.

A kite flier prepares to launch a huge kite during the Jakarta International Kite Festival. Kite-flying is a very popular hobby throughout Indonesia.

FACT FILE

● The Indonesian national language is a second language for most Indonesians, since hundreds of languages and dialects are spoken throughout the islands.

● Javanese shadow-puppet (called *wayang*) performances last for about eight hours.

● Gamelan orchestras provide a live soundtrack for almost every kind of festivity and community celebration in Java and Bali.

● In Wonosobo in central Java, men dress as women and wear masks to perform the local Lengger dance.

The Elephant Cave, on Bali, was probably carved out of rock in the 11th century to create a Hindu temple. Such decoration was a unifying tradition at a time when people on different islands spoke different languages.

Malay (and later Dutch) had for centuries been the language of traders among the islands. It also had the merit of not being Javanese, since there was always the worry that Java would dominate the rest of the country.

Bahasa Indonesia is today spoken or at least well understood in all but the most remote regions, and is promoted in the media and through the educational system. However, despite acceptance of Bahasa Indonesia as the national language, Indonesians are likely to converse within their own community in their own language or dialect. So, for example, Javanese, Sundanese and Madurese are spoken in Java, Balinese in Bali and Batak among the Batak people of Sumatra.

Most of Indonesia's hundreds of languages have relied on an oral tradition rather than a written literature. The major exception to this is classical Javanese literature, which flourished between about 900 and the decline of the mighty Majapahit kingdom in the 15th century. During this period, Hindu and Buddhist influences from India planted deep roots in Javanese culture. The great Indian Hindu epic poems the *Ramayana* and the *Mahabharata* were translated from Sanskrit (an ancient Indian language). These poems, which are widely known throughout Southeast Asia, have been adapted over time to reflect local peculiarities and are still at the heart of cultural life.

At the same time as it absorbed such Indian influences, classical Javanese literature created *kakawin* poetry. It was a court entertainment celebrating the gods, the cult of beauty and the nobility of the noble patrons who commissioned it.

The fall of the Majapahit kingdom and the rise of **Islam** led to a fusion of the two traditions and the creation of such famous works as the *Babad Tanah Jawi*. This is presented as a chronicle of Javanese life during the period of transition from the old to the new cultures, but scholars dispute its historical accuracy.

The next significant influence on the literature of Indonesia came with the Dutch presence. In particular, a young generation of European-educated writers emerged

All Indonesia Youth Congress, 1928

Both culturally and politically, Indonesians look back at this gathering in Batavia (Jakarta) in October 1928 as a decisive moment in their nation's history. Ten years earlier, the idea of replacing the name 'Dutch East Indies' with 'Indonesia' had first been discussed. During the following decade, 'Indonesia' had gained currency in the names of political parties and study groups.

The new name and the adoption of Bahasa Indonesia as a national language were major stepping stones on the path to national independence, and they were both officially proclaimed by the youth congress. The mood was perfectly captured by the pledge 'Indonesia – one nation, one people, one language', which is commemorated each year on 28 October, the anniversary of its first proclamation.

in the 1920s, centred in western Sumatra, and became the intellectual backbone of the independence movement. The first important novel written in Malay, *Sitti Nurbaya* by Marah Rusli, appeared in 1922 and enjoyed huge popularity. The young generation of novelists and poets threw their support behind the All Indonesia Youth Congress in 1928.

With the end of the Japanese occupation in 1945, Indonesian writers and intellectuals thought the time was finally right for independence, both political and cultural. Led by the flamboyant young poet Chairil Anwar, a group of writers and artists formed Angkatan 45, which translates as the 'Generation of '45'. Chairil became an icon among the idealistic young with his cry 'I want to live another thousand years'. Ironically, he died in 1949 at the age of only 27, but the values he and Angkatan 45 stood for came to symbolize the patriotic literary movement that flourished during the Sukarno era. Whatever the economic verdict on the long Suharto years, the political repression that occurred during that time brought a halt to the **radicalism** and **idealism** associated with Angkatan 45.

Each of the latticed dome-shaped structures (called stupas) on the top of the temple of Borobudur contain an image of the Buddha.

Art and architecture

The great glory of Indonesian art and architecture is reflected in the majestic temples and palaces of central and eastern Java. These monuments are visible reminders of the great Indian-inspired civilizations that ruled Java for hundreds of years, before giving way first to Islamic and later to Dutch influence and power.

This Classical Age saw the building of the great Buddhist temple of Borobudur and the Hindu complex at Prambanan. Both these glorious

monuments were erected during the 9th and 10th centuries – during the European Dark Ages. They and the many other wonderful shrines (*candis*) that grace the Java landscape are undoubtedly influenced by Indian religion and philosophy. At the same time, they are distinctively Javanese and represent a great artistic flowering during the Classical Age.

The Classical Age is divided chronologically between the Central Javanese period and the East Javanese period. Borobudur and Prambanan represent the Central Java period, which ended abruptly around 929 when Mount Merapi erupted. A great migration to the fertile lands of east Java followed, and for the next 600 years, this remained the centre of Javanese religion and culture. The *candis* from this later period were not built on such a magnificent scale as Borobudur and Prambanan, but the finest of them display very beautiful craftsmanship.

The Hindu temple of Prambanan was built during the Central Java period in the 10th century. Its huge tiered towers are dedicated to the Hindu gods Siva, Brahma and Vishnu.

It takes great skill to carve the intricate patterns on shadow puppets. Shadow-puppet performances last for many hours and are social events that whole families, including children, attend.

With the fall of the Majapahit **dynasty** in 1527, temple-building came to an end, to be replaced by the construction of mosques. The new Islamic rulers felt no need to reject existing styles, however, and Javanese mosques – like so many aspects of Javanese life – became a unique blend of the old and the new. Java became, and remains, an Islamic society constructed upon solid Hindu and Buddhist foundations.

Javanese shadow-puppet theatre

The Javanese word '*wayang*' means 'shadow', and *wayang kulit* is a theatrical performance in which shadow images of two-dimensional puppets are projected on a backlit screen. As developed in central Java, *wayang kulit* is one of the oldest continuing traditions of story-telling in the world. It is one of the real highlights of Javanese life, and, with local modifications, this world-famous shadow puppetry is just as popular and culturally significant in Bali. *Wayang kulit* performances are designed not only to entertain, but also to explain history and philosophy and the great creation myths.

Most *wayang kulit* performances and the characters the puppets represent are based on the Indian epic poems the *Ramayana* and the *Mahabharata*. Over time, these epics were modified to take account of the very different circumstances of life in Java, but they retain the spirit of the originals. Both epics are thousands of verses long, so only certain parts are staged at one time. Even so, the performances are exceedingly long compared to those of Western theatre. They usually begin at 8 or 9 in the evening and run right through without a break till dawn.

Wayang kulit performances are the high point of religious festivals and public holidays in towns and villages, and a feature of weddings and birth celebrations. In Bali, *wayang kulit* performances may also be staged at cremations.

While it is the puppet characters that the audience delights in, it is obviously the puppet master who carries the show. The *dalang*, as he is known, must surely be the hardest working and most versatile entertainer in the world. He sits near the screen and moves the puppets around to illustrate the story he is telling. He not only narrates the story but sings and cracks jokes, and speaks the dialogue for all the characters, too. And somehow or other amid all this hubub, he manages to conduct a gamelan orchestra of maybe twenty or more instruments. Not surprisingly the best *dalangs* are greatly revered, as philosophical teachers and gurus as much as entertainers.

Puppet-making

The fabulous *wayang kulit* puppets are made from leather ('*kulit*' means 'leather'). Water-buffalo hide is matured for up to ten years to get it dry and stiff enough for the purpose. The hide is then carved and decorated with very intricate patterns made of tiny holes, and painted. The puppet is supported by a rod of buffalo horn running down the centre, while smaller rods enable the *dalang* to move the arms and legs.

The skill of the puppet maker is judged on the intricacy and beauty of the carving and decorating of the puppets, which are meant to represent exaggerated character types. They all have long necks and arms, but there is an extraordinary variety of eye, nose and mouth shapes, all of which are recognizable to a knowledgeable audience. An especially well-made puppet is said to have *guna* (a quality that makes its character seem more real). *Guna* increases with age, so old puppets are more valuable.

A gamelan orchestra is made up almost entirely of percussion instruments, although sometimes bamboo flutes are included.

Music and dance

In 1580, the great English explorer and adventurer Sir Francis Drake visited Java on his epic voyage around the world. He was particularly impressed by the local music, 'of a very strange kind, pleasant and delightful'.

The word 'gamelan' refers to the traditional Javanese ensemble of tuned percussion instruments and also to the music the ensemble makes. The ensemble consists of gongs, drums, chimes, cymbals and metallophones (similar to xylophones), although all this percussion can be balanced with flutes and stringed instruments. The bars of the gamelan instruments can be made of bronze, brass or iron, while the instrument frames are made of intricately carved and painted wood. The largest and finest bronze gamelans are found in the royal palaces of central Java, which are at the heart of all Javanese art and culture.

A large-scale gamelan may consist of 30 musicians, all of whom can play any of the instruments. The large gongs are at the back of the ensemble, the metallo-phones in the centre and the more delicate-sounding instruments such as zithers and flutes are at the front.

Gamelan music is a frequent companion to dance performances, and there is a huge variety of traditional dance styles in Indonesia. Java is famous for its dance academies, and Bali has a rich tradition of dances. These include the well-known Kecak dance, which tells the tale of the Hindu epic the *Ramayana*, and the elegant Legong dance, of which there are many forms. Kali-mantan has the Mandau dance, with knives and shields.

Gamelan music is not only an essential part of the all-night *wayang kulit* shadow-puppet performances. It is also a feature of all festivals and festivities in every town and village in Java and Bali.

EVERYDAY LIFE

Life in Indonesia's cities is very different from that of the remote countryside. While a person living in Jakarta might work in an air-conditioned office and use a computer every day, a farmer in a remote village in Kalimantan has probably never even seen a computer.

Food and drink

Indonesian cuisine reflects the nation's complex cultural history. Because of its location on the great trade routes between Asia and Europe, Indonesia always attracted traders who were eager to exploit the riches of the Spice Islands (see page 58). In the course of their trading, these foreigners introduced elements of their own native cuisines – curries and cucumbers from India, the wok and stir-fry technique from China and kebabs from the Middle East. Later on, Europeans brought tomatoes and other exotic foods from the Americas, such as papaya and squash. So many elements from so many far-flung places have gone into Indonesian cuisine that it really is a taste of the world.

Indonesian food bears a resemblance to Indian and Thai food. Fittingly, since it was the spice trade that made Indonesia famous, spices figure prominently in the food. Chillies, coriander, turmeric, cumin, cardamom, galangal (a relative of ginger) and lemon grass are all familiar flavours in many different combinations.

Village women in Bali gather to harvest a neighbour's rice. Traditionally, each woman will be rewarded with rice for her help.

Nutmeg and cloves, which were at the very heart of the old spice trade, are used much more commonly in medicines than in cooking in Indonesia.

Along with spices, coconut milk and coconut cream feature heavily in Indonesian cooking, both to tame the fiery heat of the chillies and to contribute the sweet, creamy flavour that is unique to coconut products. Coconut milk is also used in drinks.

Kalimantan shrimp

Indonesian cuisine varies considerably from region to region, but there are common themes running through it. This dish, which is attributed to Kalimantan, has many features typical of Indonesian food: rice, spices, seafood. It is extremely easy to prepare – and absolutely delicious. The only ingredient that may not be familiar is tamarind paste. Tamarind is an important ingredient in both Asian and Latin American recipes. Its sour, fruity taste blends well with the fiery flavour of chillies. It can usually be bought as a bottled paste.

You will need:

1 tbsp tamarind paste
50 ml (2 fl oz) water
1 kg (2 lb) raw shrimp, peeled and deveined
2 tbsp olive oil
1 clove garlic, sliced
4 medium-sized red chilli peppers, sliced
1 shallot, sliced
1 tbsp brown sugar
3 cm (1 in) piece ginger, chopped
1 medium-sized tomato, chopped
1 tsp sea salt
rice

Method:

Mix the tamarind paste with water. Sauté the shrimp in half the oil over a moderate heat for 2 minutes. In a food processor (or using a pestle and mortar), blend the garlic, chilli peppers, shallot, sugar, tamarind mixture, ginger, tomato and salt to form a paste. Heat the remaining oil in a pan and stir-fry the paste over a moderate heat for 3–4 minutes. Add the shrimp and cook for a further 2 minutes. Serve with steamed or boiled rice.

Rice is the staple cereal, and Indonesians prefer highly polished long-grain rice. Cooked one way or another – steamed, boiled, fried – rice is eaten at breakfast, lunch and dinner.

Roasted peanuts and peanut paste also feature prominently, along with peanut oil, the main cooking oil.

Meals are served with soya sauce and one or more *sambals* – spice relishes that are served as garnishes or side dishes. Some of the tastiest are fresh salsa-like mixtures, but they can be very hot and fiery, so newcomers to Indonesian food are warned to be cautious. *Sambal ulek*, which is a favourite found almost everywhere,

Religious life

Virtually everybody in Indonesia claims to belong to one religion or another. Of the nation's 206 million population, 88% say they are Muslim, which makes Indonesia the world's largest Muslim nation. Another 9 per cent are Christian (Protestants, 6 per cent; Roman Catholics, 3 per cent), while 2 per cent are Hindu and 1 per cent is Buddhist.

However, these statistics conceal important features about religious belief and practice in Indonesia. Many Muslims believe in much of the mystical tradition of **Hinduism** and **Buddhism**, as well as in elements of folk Islam. And Indonesians of all religions are likely to believe also in magic potions, spiritualism, nature gods and so on – such beliefs are described by the blanket term 'animism'.

The 1945 Constitution has great significance for Indonesians. It not only expresses the ideals and goals of independence, but it was also inspired by philosophical principles that underlie the Indonesian approach to life, including promoting religious tolerance. Pancasila (the five principles upon which the Republic of Indonesia is founded) refers to a belief in 'the one and only God'. In practice, the principle has been stretched to include Hindu and Buddhist beliefs as well as Muslim and Christian ones.

From the days of independence after World War Two (1939–45) to the present, every Indonesian government has resisted pressure to make Indonesia an Islamic state, including both presidents Sukarno and Suharto. They wanted to keep religion and politics separate and tried to stamp out religious intolerance.

is a blisteringly hot chilli relish made of ground red chillies, salt, sugar and vinegar.

Fish is the staple food in Indonesia, and the tropical waters around the archipelago are home to a wonderful variety of fish and seafood. Fish market stalls groan under the weight of tuna and carp, shrimps and prawns, crabs and lobsters. Chicken and beef are eaten too and feature in many Indonesian dishes. Although the Hindu Balinese and the urban Chinese eat pork, the overwhelming majority of **Muslim** Indonesians do not eat pork. They do, however, consume plenty of goat meat.

Education

Approximately 88 per cent of Indonesians aged fifteen or over can read and write, but this relatively high literacy rate flatters a ramshackle education system. State schooling is not free in Indonesia, and the country has the fourth lowest expenditure on education in the world.

Children start school when they are seven and spend six years at primary school before going to secondary school. Although school fees are low, some families have difficulty paying for their children's uniforms and books on top of the fees. The very poor cannot afford to send their children to school at all and send them out to work instead. Attendance rates at primary and secondary school have dropped dramatically since the start of the economic crisis in Indonesia (see page 83), as more and more families fall into poverty.

The private schools, which are often run by churches and mosques, offer better standards of education. Their fees are higher than those of the state schools, however, and only wealthy families can afford to send their children to these schools.

A university education is very expensive and few can afford to go. The foremost universities and colleges are located in Java, although there are other universities in other provinces. The largest and most prestigious university is Jakarta's University of Indonesia (UI).

'Give a person a patch of land on which to grow rice and a stretch of water in which to fish, and he (or she) will be content for life.' Indonesian saying

EDUCATIONAL ATTENDANCE

university and college	8.1%
secondary school	48.3%
primary school	95.5%

source: Government of Indonesia

Sport and leisure

Badminton is very popular throughout Indonesia, and there are courts everywhere. These boys are playing on a court that has been erected in a Balinese temple.

Indonesians play a wide variety of sports, including football. While there are few full-time professional football players, teams are sponsored by corporations that provide employment for their players. Tennis is popular, too, and Indonesian tennis teams win many regional competitions. It is badminton, however, that really gets Indonesians excited. For decades, Indonesians, men and women alike have been top contenders for badminton titles at the very highest international levels. They brought home four medals including a gold from the Olympic Games at Atlanta in 1996, and they regularly battle it out with the Chinese at the World Championships. One of the greatest badminton players of all time was the Indonesian Rudy Hartono (born 1949). For seven consecutive years from 1968, and again in 1976, he won the All England Men's Singles Championship, which is the badminton equivalent of winning a Wimbledon tennis title.

How to say ...

Bahasa Indonesia is written in Roman script, so it looks familiar to Westerners. The grammar is simple, which means that visitors find the language quite easy to speak on a basic level. Word order is the same as it is in English (subject-verb-object). Verbs have no tenses (such as past or future) and there are no articles (such as 'the' or 'a'). Most words are pronounced the way they look, with the stress on the second-to-last syllable.

Here are a few common words and phrases.

What is your name?   *Siapa nama anda?*
My name is ...   *Nama saya...*
Where do you come from?   *Dari mana?*
I come from ...   *Saya dari ...*
Do you Speak English?   *Bisa bicara bahasa Inggris?*
I [don't] understand   *Saya [tidak] mengerti*
Yes/No   *Ya/Tidak*
Please   *Tolong*
Thank you   *Terima kasih*
You're welcome   *Sama sama* or *kembali*
Excuse me   *Ma'af*
How are you?   *Apa kabar?*
I'm fine   *Kabar baik*
Good morning (up to 11 AM)   *Selamat pagi*
Good day (11 AM–3 PM)   *Selamat siang*
Good afternoon (3 PM–dusk)   *Selamat sore*
Good evening (after dark)   *Selamat malam*

Good night   *Selamat tidur*
See you later   *Sampai jumpa lagi*
Where is the ...?   *Dimana ...?*
airport   *lapangan terbang*
train station   *stasiun kereta api*
bus station   *stasiun bis*
police station   *stasiun polisi*
bank   *bank*
post office   *kantor pos*
chemist   *apotik*
tourist office   *kantor turis*
Is it far?   *Jauh?*
I want to buy a ticket to ...   *Saya mau beli karcis ke ...*

Numbers:

one   *satu*
two   *dua*
three   *tiga*
four   *empat*
five   *lima*
six   *enam*
seven   *tujuh*
eight   *delapan*
nine   *sembilan*
ten   *sepuluh*

Days of the week:

Monday   *Hari Senin*
Tuesday   *Hari Selasa*
Wednesday   *Hari Rabu*
Thursday   *Hari Kamis*
Friday   *Hari Jumat*
Saturday   *Hari Sabtu*
Sunday   *Hari Minggu*

There are many traditional games and sports enjoyed throughout the country. Boat-racing and surf-boarding are very popular, while kite-flying is almost a national institution. The island of Madura is famous for its annual festival of bull-racing, and cock-fighting has a large following in Bali.

One of the most exciting and explosive team games in the world, *sepak takraw*, is widely played all over Southeast Asia, including in Indonesia. Its English name is kick volleyball. As the name suggests, it is like volleyball except that the ball cannot be played with the hands or arms. Instead, the players use their knees, shoulders, head and of course feet to propel the ball across the net into the opponents' court. *Sepak takraw* is played on a badminton court and uses a badminton net. This is perfect for Indonesia since badminton is the nation's favourite sport and there are courts everywhere.

The government-sponsored National Sports Day falls on 9 September. It goes back to pre-independence days and is celebrated as a symbol of Indonesian unity.

Holidays and festivals

There are many religious holidays in Indonesia throughout the year (see box opposite). Islamic and Buddhist festivals are fixed according to the lunar calendar (the various phases of the moon), so they move back between ten and twelve days (in the Western calendar) each year. All start at sundown the evening before the date given.

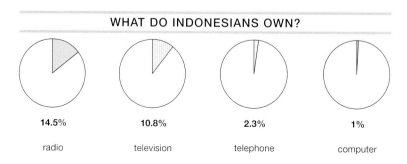

WHAT DO INDONESIANS OWN?

| 14.5% | 10.8% | 2.3% | 1% |
| radio | television | telephone | computer |

source: Government of Indonesia

Important holidays and festivals

1 January – New Year's Day (Tahun Baru). New Year's Eve has a lively carnival atmosphere with street parades, fireworks and music.

Late winter – Chinese New Year. This is not an official holiday, but it is celebrated by the large Chinese population in Indonesia. The climax is the spectacular dragon and lion dance to ward off evil for the coming year.

February – Festival of Sacrifice (Eid al-Adha). This commemorates the willingness of the biblical prophet Abraham to sacrifice his son in response to God's command. Those who can slaughter an animal (sheep, goat or cow), eat some of the meat and distribute the rest to the poor.

Late winter – Islamic New Year (Muharram). This marks the first day of the Muslim calendar and commemorates the Prophet Muhammad's journey from Mecca to Medina in 622.

March or April – Hindu New Year (Nyepi). Balinese Hindus mark their new year with meditation rather than parties. Everything closes down for the day. People stay at home, do no work and spend the day quietly.

April Good Friday.

Spring – Birth of the Prophet (Mawlid al-Nabi). A month of celebrations commemorate Muhammad's birth in 571.

May – Buddha's birthday (Waisak). The main event is in central Java, where a procession of Buddhist monks makes its way to the shrine at Borobudur.

17 August – Independence Day. The most important national celebration continues for the best part of a month.

9 September – National Sports Day. Celebrated as a symbol of national unity.

Late summer – Ascension of the Prophet (Lailat al-Miraj). This commemorates the Prophet's ascension into the seven heavens and his return to the Earth.

Autumn – First day of Ramadan (Awal Ramadan). Muslims fast from sunrise to sunset during the month of Ramadan.

Late autumn – Feast of the Fast Breaking (Eid-al-Fitr). The end of Ramadan begins three days of celebration when gifts are exchanged and people get together for feasting.

25 December – Christmas Day.

The future

'Let us look to the future and unite to restore our life and dignity as a nation.'

President Megawati Sukarnoputri,
after being sworn in as Indonesia's fifth president, 23 July 2001

It is difficult to cast a future for Indonesia without first looking at the medium and long-term effects of the Bali bombings of 2002. In the short term, the effects were predictably terrible, with the Bali tourist industry grinding to a halt overnight. While in early 2003 there were signs of recovery, most observers agree that Bali's reputation as a carefree paradise for Westerners has been irreparably damaged.

The damage to Bali's reputation is only partly due to the shocking images left by the bombing. The unmistakable message of the **atrocity** was that, for terrorists of this kind, tourists are not just fair game but are a prime target. The bombings also drew attention to the fact that Indonesia has a poor record for ensuring people's safety and a reputation for religious and social violence.

Just a few months before the Bali bombings, a bomb attack on a crowded bus on the island of Sulawesi left four dead. The bomb was probably planted by Islamic extremists trying to sabotage a fragile ceasefire between rival **Muslim** and Christian gangs, who have been at each others' throats for years.

On the neighbouring islands of Maluku, also in 2002, gunmen shot dead fourteen Christians in the village of Soya. The killers are believed to have been members of the Muslim extremist group Laskar Jihad. The group rejects the idea of religious tolerance and has

During the 1998 riots in Jakarta, Chinese businesses were targeted.

Historically, there has been much resentment against the Chinese in Indonesia.

called instead for a holy war against Maluku's large Christian population.

The Sumatran province of Aceh remains the scene of a fierce **guerrilla** independence struggle. Foreigners are strongly warned against going there, and they are warned off going to Papua for the same reason. Before East Timor became independent in 2002, the name 'Timor' had long been a byword for blood-letting.

In Java, anti-Western sentiment is not far below the surface. The war in Iraq in early 2003 intensified anger against coalition partners – the UK, the USA and Australia. Visitors were advised to stay well clear of demonstrations, and mob violence and **vigilante** action frequently scarred the streets of Jakarta.

Despite the wonderful attractions of the Indonesian landscape, its peoples and its cultures, the security concerns and continuing conflicts mean that tourists may be slow to return to Indonesia.

THE SUHARTO LEGACY

While tourism is a vital component of Bali's economy, it does not play such a significant part in Indonesia's economy as a whole. And it is within the wider economy that the nation's future will be shaped.

Indonesia is in the middle of transforming itself after the 32-year period of political stagnation under the iron rule of General Suharto. Since his fall from power in 1998, the nation under his democratically elected successors has been trying to grapple with the mess the old dictator left behind. The worst of his legacy is neatly expressed by the letters 'KKN', which translate as '**corruption, collusion** and **nepotism**'.

Corruption infected every aspect of business and government activity in the Suharto years, and stamping it out will be a long and difficult task. By 2003, many legal and economic reforms had been put in place as the necessary price for help from the World Bank and the International Monetary Fund (IMF). However, the

enormous and deeply conservative bureaucracy – and the habits of a lifetime – remain a huge obstacle to progress. Traditionally, public officials were poorly paid and expected to pick the public pocket – through bribes and other payments – to supplement their low salaries. Big salary increases have gone some way to improving this situation, but it will take a long time to break the bad habits and create the morale needed for providing proper public services.

These are daunting problems that face Indonesia, yet there is reason for guarded optimism. Many Indonesians are eager to shake off the nation's 'Third World' image, to improve its economic performance and to emerge in the 21st century as a forward-looking **democracy**. Many hoped that the outcome of the presidential elections would go some way to achieving these goals. The challenge is to do that while preserving the priceless cultural and religious heritage that is unique to this fascinating corner of the world.

A boy from one of Jakarta's shanty towns enjoys a computer lesson. He is taking part in a project funded by an international software company to teach children from poor families how to use a computer. Much of Indonesia's future success as a prosperous democracy will depend on children from all backgrounds having the opportunity to learn.

Almanac

POLITICAL

country name:
official form: Republic of Indonesia
short form: Indonesia
local long form: Republik Indonesia
local short form: Indonesia

nationality:
noun: Indonesian(s)
adjective: Indonesian

official language: Bahasa Indonesia

capital city: Jakarta

type of government: republic

suffrage (voting rights):
everyone seventeen years and
over and married persons of
any age

independence: 17 August 1945

national anthem: 'Indonesia Raya'

national holiday:
17 August (Independence Day)

flag:

GEOGRAPHICAL

location: Southeast Asia, archipelago
between the Indian Ocean and
the Pacific Ocean

climate: tropical; hot, humid; more
moderate in highlands

total area: 1,919,440 sq km
(741,096 sq miles)
land: 95%
water: 5%

coastline: 54,716 km (34,000 miles)

terrain: mostly coastal lowlands; larger
islands have interior mountains

highest point: Puncak Jaya
5030 m (16,503 ft)

lowest point: Indian Ocean, 0 m

land use (2003 est.):
arable land: 9.9%
permanent crops: 7.2%
other uses: 82.9%

natural resources: petroleum, tin,
natural gas, nickel, timber,
bauxite, copper, fertile soils,
coal, gold, silver

natural hazards: occasional floods, severe droughts, tsunamis, earthquakes, volcanoes, forest fires

POPULATION

population (2003 est.): 234.9 million

population growth rate (2003 est.): 1.52%

birth rate (2003 est.): 21.4 births per 1000 of the population

death rate (2003 est.): 6.26 deaths per 1000 of the population

sex ratio (2003 est.): 105 males per 100 females

total fertility rate (2003 est.): 2.59 children born per woman

infant mortality rate (2003 est.): 38.1 deaths per 1000 live births

life expectancy at birth (2003 est.): total population: 68.9 years male: 66.5 years female: 71.5 years

literacy: total population: 88% male: 92.9% female: 84.1%

ECONOMY

currency: Rupiah (Rp); 1 Rupiah = 100 sen

exchange rate (2003): £1 = Rp 13,743

gross domestic product (2002): £438,000 million

gross domestic product by sectors: agriculture: 17% industry: 41% services: 42%

GDP per capita (2002): £456

average annual growth rate (1990–2000): 4.6%

average annual inflation rate (2002): 11.9%

unemployment rate (2002): 11%

exports (2002): £34,500 million

imports (2002): £21,200 million

aid given (1997–2000): £26,875 million

Human Development Index
(an index scaled from 0 to 100 combining statistics indicating adult literacy, years of schooling, life expectancy and income levels)**:**
67.7 (UK 92.3)

TIMELINE—INDONESIA

World History

Indonesian History

c.10,000 BC

c.10,000 Invention of bow and arrow

c.6000 Rice cultivation starts in Asia

ca. 2000 Settlers start to practice agriculture around the Indonesian Archipelago

c.700 BC

c.563 Birth of the Buddha

551 Birth of the Chinese thinker Confucius

c.AD 100

330 Constantinople becomes capital of the Eastern Roman (Byzantine) empire

c.570 Birth of Muhammad in Mecca

c.100 Trade and travel between the islands and mainland Asia is established

c.400–500 Hindu kingdoms spread their influence over the archipelago

c.700–800 Muslim Indian traders begin spreading Islam

639 Muslim armies conquer the southern territories of the Byzantine empire

618–907 China has a Golden Age of art and literature under the Tang dynasty

1526 Foundation of Mughal empire in India

1492 Columbus lands in America

1368 Foundation of the Ming dynasty in China

1151 First use of explosives in war by China

1595 Dutch expedtion, led by Cornelius de Houtman, reaches the archipelago

1511 Portuguese expedition captures the Muslim port of Malaka

c.1500

1478 Muslim state of Demak overwhelms Majapahit control; last Hindu prince flees to Bali

c.1100

c.750–950 Buddhist Sailendra dynasty prospers

c.600–1400 Buddhist kingdom of Srivijaya in Sumatra and Hindu kingdom of Majapahit in eastern Java flourish

c.1600

1602 Dutch East India Company is founded; a monopoly on Indonesian exports to Europe is established

2001 The World Trade Center and the Pentagon in the USA are attacked by planes flown by al-Qaeda terrorists

2002 A terrorist bomb explodes on the island of Bali, killing more than 200 people

1650–1700 Explosion of observational science in Europe leads to the new physics, discovery of microscopic life and blood circulation

1619 Jayakarta (Jakarta) falls to the Dutch and is renamed Batavia

2000 The West celebrates the Millennium – 2000 years since the birth of Christ

2001 Megawati Sukarnoputri becomes president

1799 Dutch East India Company is disbanded; Indonesia becomes a formal part of the Dutch colonial empire

1989 Communism collapses in eastern Europe

1968–98 General Sukarno serves six five-year terms back to back as president

1775–83 American War of Independence

1963–75 The Vietnam War

1949 Indonesia officially achieves independence

c.1950

1949 Communists take power in China

1945 Achmed Sukarno proclaims Indonesia a republic

c.1800

1815 French emperor Napoleon is defeated at Waterloo

1821–37 Padri War: conflict in Sumatra between Muslim reformers, the local Islamic community and the Dutch

1939–45 World War Two

1942–45 The Japanese invade and occupy Indonesia

1839–60 The Opium Wars between China and Britain; China is forced to make huge trading concessions

1825–30 Java War: Prince Diponegoro declares a holy war on the Dutch

1927 Formation of the Indonesian Nationalist Party, PNI, led by Achmed Sukarno

1861–65 American Civil War

1891 Java Man is discovered

1914–18 World War One

1911 Imperial rule ends in China

1917 Compulsory coffee cultivation ends

c. 1900

Glossary

atoll ring-shaped island or reef surrounding a lagoon

atom bomb extremely powerful bomb that uses the energy released when the nucleus of an atom is split

atrocity extremely wicked act or thing

Buddhism religion of eastern and central Asia based on the teachings of the prophet Siddartha Gautama (the Buddha)

candi small stone Hindu shrine, usually tiered

cannibalism practice of eating human flesh

cash crops crops such as coffee grown for export to generate foreign currency, not for domestic consumption

cassowary large flightless bird

caste person's social level, determined by their birth

civet type of wild cat

cockatoo type of parrot, often with a large crest

collusion secret and fraudulent agreements between people or groups

colonialism control of one country or people by another

communism political system in which goods and land are owned by everyone and there is no private property

corruption use of practices such as bribery; wickedness

counter-insurgency actions used against a revolt or rebellion

coup d'état sudden overthrow of the government by a small group, often military

creationism belief that the world was created by God (not by evolution)

democracy country or process in which the people choose their government by election, and in which they hold supreme power

dialect regional variation of a national language

dynasty succession of rulers who all belong to the same family

echidna spiny egg-laying mammal

elite select group or class

equatorial of or near the equator

ethical morally correct; honourable

ethnic group a racial or linguistic group

feudalism medieval system of government, in which peasants work for and provide services to landowners

fundamentalism strict adherence to the basic beliefs of a religion, usually involving the exclusion of other beliefs

gamelan Indonesian orchestra, mainly made up of percussion instruments; also the music

gross national product (GNP) total value of goods and services produced by the people of a country during a period, usually a year

guerilla war small, independently acting groups engaged in warfare

Hinduism historic religion of India, based on a large number of gods and originating in the second millennium BC

humanitarian describes person or group that promotes human welfare or humane action

idealism behaviour or thought that follows ideals or principles

imperialism practice of conquering other countries to form an empire

indigenous belonging to a region or country; native

Islam religion founded in Arabia in the 7th century and based on the teachings of Muhammad

magma liquid or molten rock deep in the Earth

mangrove tropical tree that grows in swamps or shallow water

marsupials mammals that give birth to underdeveloped young that climb into their mothers' pouches to continue growing

militia group of armed citizens, rather than professional soldiers

monopoly exclusive control over something

monsoon period of intense rainfall occurring at the same time every year

Muslim follower of the teachings of Islam

nationalism people's sense of belonging to a nation; also the belief that a nation should be independent of, and sometimes superior to, other nations

naturalist person who studies nature

nepotism favouritism shown to relatives

palaeontologist person who studies early geological periods through fossil remains

platypus aquatic, egg-laying mammal

possum tree-dwelling marsupial

primates humans, apes and monkeys as a group

quarantine isolation to prevent the spread of disease or pests

radicalism political philosophy that promotes extreme change in society

savannah large area of arid grassland with sparse trees and bushes

scorched-earth policy to burn and destroy an area before handing it over to the enemy

socialism political theory that teaches that society as a whole should be in control of a country's resources and businesses

sultanate land ruled by a sultan, a Muslim ruler

vigilante member of an informal group that keeps order and punishes crime

zealot fanatic, person who is passionately devoted to a cause or thing

Bibliography

Major sources used for this book
The Rough Guide to Indonesia (Rough Guides, 2003, 2nd edn)
Turner, Peter et al., *Indonesia* (Lonely Planet Publications, 2000, 6th edn)

General further reading
Bacon, Derek, *Culture Shock: Jakarta at Your Door* (Graphic Arts Center Publishing Co., 1999)
Bourchier, David and Hadiz, Vedi (eds), *Indonesian Politics and Society: A Reader* (Routledge, 2001)
Cribb, Robert, *Historical Atlas of Indonesia* (Curzon, 1999)
Ricklefs, M. C., *A History of Modern Indonesia Since c.1200* (Stanford University Press, 2002)

Further reading about Indonesia
Daws, Gavan and Fujita, Marty, *Archipelago: Islands of Indonesia* (University of California Press, 1999)

Friend, Theodore, *Indonesian Destinies* (Belknap Press, 2003)
Gelman Taylor, Jean, *Indonesia: Peoples and Histories* (Yale University Press, 2003)
Ingram, William, *A Little Bit One o'Clock: Living with a Balinese family* (Ersania Books, 1998)
Tantri, K'tut, *Revolt in Paradise* (Clarkson N. Potter, 1990)
Toer, Pramaoedya Ananta, *Tales from Djakarta* (Cornell University, 1999)
Toer, Pramaoedya Ananta, *The Mute's Soliloquy: A Memoir* (Hyperion, 1999)

Some websites about Indonesia
CIA World Factbook
www.cia.gov/cia/publications/factbook/geos/id.html
Worldwide directory of Indonesia
www.externalharddrive.com/countries/indonesia.html

Index

Page numbers in *italics* refer to pictures or their captions.

A

agriculture 26, 27, 83, 87–9, 88
airports 93, 96
Albuquerque, Alfonso d' 59
All Indonesia Youth Congress (1928) 99, 101
Ambon 37
Angkatan 45 102
animism 110
arts 99–107
Asmat 35

B

Bali 17–22, 26, 56, 100
Bali bombings 94–5, 94, 95, 97, 117
Balikpapan 89
Banda Islands 33, 59
Bandung 89
Banten 57
Batak people 23, 97
Batavia 43–4, 43, 60, 61, 66
batik 92, 92
birds 14, 36, 36, 47
bird sanctuaries 14
bombs, terrorist 22, 94–5, 94, 95, 97, 117
Borobudur 47, 53, 53, 55, 102
British, the 71–2, 73, 74
Buddhism 11, 47, 53, 55, 101, 102–3, 102, 110
bull-racing 21, 21

C

cannibalism 23
caves 34, 100
child labor 91
Chinese, the 117
cigarettes 88–9
cities 11, 42–7
Classical Age 51–5, 103
climate 34–7, 37
coal 85–7
Coen, Jan Pieterszoon 60
colonial era 62–8
Columbus, Christopher 49, 58
communism 68, 68, 69, 75–6
Communist Party, Indonesian (PKI) 68, 69, 75, 76
computers 119
Constitution (1945) 80
copper 84
corruption 83, 93, 118
crops 83
cultivation system 64

D

dance 99, 107
Dani people 38
Dayaks 30
Deer Island 28
deforestation 41, 86, 86
Dekker, E.F.E. Douwes 69
democracy, guided 73, 74
Denpasar 89
Deventer, C.T. van 67–8
Diponegoro, Prince 62, 63
Dubois, Eugene 49, 50
Dutch, the 43–4, 43, 49, 57, 59–62, 60, 62–8, 72, 74
Dutch East India Company 58, 59–60, 62
Dutch East Indies 8, 62, 66–7
dye, indigo 64

E

earthquakes 29
East Indies 58
East Timor 77, 78
economy 83–97
education 111, 111, 119
elections (1999) 81, 81
elephants, Asian 39
energy sources 85
ethical policy, the 67–8
ethnic groups 8, 11
exports 84, 91, 91

F

flag 8, 8
Flores 29, 29
flowers 41, 41
food and drink 107–11
foreign arrivals 96
future, the 117–19

G

Gajah Mada 54
gamelan music 99, 106–7, 106
gas, natural 85
gold 87, 87
Golden Age, Java's 55
government 80–1, 80, 81
gross national product (GNP) 83
guided democracy 73, 74
Gunung Agung 20
Gunung Leuser National Park 24–5, 25, 39

H

Habibie, B.J. 79
Hatta, Muhammad 69, 72
Hayam Wuruk 54
head-hunters 30
Hinduism 11, 22, 47, 51, 53–4, 56, 100, 101, 102–3, 103
history 49–79
holidays and festivals 114–15
House of Representatives 80
houses 97
Houtman, Cornelius de 59
humans, prehistoric 49–51

I

imports *84*, 91, *91*
independence *49*, 70–3
Indonesian Democratic Party
   of Struggle 81
Indonesian Nationalist Party
   69
industry 89–93, *89*
International Monetary Fund
   (IMF) 78–9, 83–4, 91
Irian Jaya 34, 74
Islam and Muslims 7, 11, 55–6,
   101, 104, 110
islands 13, 26–30, 32–4

J

Jakarta 7, *37*, 42–5, *44* (map),
   65, 66, 89, *117*
Japanese occupation 70, *71*
Java 7, 9, *13*, 14–16, 20, *49*,
   57, 64, 103, 118
Java Man 49, 50, *50*
Java War 62–3, 69
Jayapura 89

K

Kalimantan 9, 30
Kelimutu *29*
Kendari *71*
kite-flying 99
Komodo dragons 31, *31*
Komodo Island 28, 31
konfrontasi 74–5
Krakatau 18–19, *18*, *19*
kretek 88–9
Kupang 89
Kuta 22, 94, *94*
Kutei 51

L

land use *85*, 87
language 113
languages 7, 10, 99–100
Laskar Jihad 117–18
liberal policy, the 64–5
life, everyday 107–15
literature 100–1
logging, illegal 86

Lombok 26–7, *27*, 56

M

Madura Island 21
Majapahit dynasty *52*, 54–5
Makassar 89
malnutrition 117
Maluku 117–18
Maluku archipelago 33–4
Manado 35–7, 89
maps *15*, 85
Maros caves 34
Medan 89
minerals *84*, *85*, 87
mining 84
Moluccas (Maluku) 33, 58, *58*
money 8, *8*
monsoons 35
motto, national 13
mountains 13, 16, *17*, 34
music 99, 106–7, *106*

N

name 8
national anthem 9
nationalism 63, 68–70
National Monument *44*
national parks 16, 20, 24–5,
   30, 39, 40
New Guinea 34
New Order 76–7
Nias Island 16
Nusa Tenggara 26–30
nutmeg *33*

O

oil 85, 89–90, *90*
orangutans 24–5, *25*, 39
orchids *41*

P

Padang 89
Padri 63
Padri War 63, 69
paintings, cave 34
Palembang 51, 89
Pancasila 11, 80

Pangrango, Mount 65
Papua 9, 34, *35*, *38*, 40, *84*

People's Consultative Assembly
   80–1, *80*
PKI 68, 69, 75, 76
plantations 88
plants 40–1, *41*
PNI 69
poems 101
Pontianak 89
population 8–9, *10*
ports 96
Portuguese, the 42–3, 59
poverty 117
Prambanan 102–3, *103*
president 80
provinces and regions 14–34,
   22 (map)
Pulau Dua 14
Pulau Menjangan 28
Puncak Jaya 34
puppets, shadow 99, 104–5,
   104

R

Raffles, Sir Thomas Stamford
   61, *61*, 62
rafflesia 41
railways 93–6, *93*
rainforests 41, 85, 86
religion 10–11, *11*, 110
resources, natural 84–7, *84*
rhinoceroses, Javan 20
rice fields 22, 26, 27, 88, *88*
Ring of Fire 13, 17, 29
roads 93, *93*
Rockefeller, Michael 39
rubber 88

S

Sailendra dynasty 52–3
Samosir 23
Sanjaya dynasty 53–4
Semarang 89
sepak takraw 114
smoking 88–9
Sneevliet, Hendricus 69
Soviet Union 74–5

Spice Islands 33, 49, 58
spices *33*, *56*, *57–8*, *59*, 108
sport 112–14, *112*
Srivijaya kingdom 51–2, *52*
Suharto, General 75, *76–9*, *77*, 79, 86, 118
Sukarno, Achmed 69, *70*, *72*, *73–5*, *75*, 80
Sukarnoputri, Megawati 79, 81
Sulawesi 32, *32*, 34, *71*, *83*, 117
Sumatra 16–17, 23, 37, 41, *97*, 118
Sumba 29–30
Sumbawa 27–8
Sunda Kelapa 42, *43*
Surabaya 49, 72
swamps, mangrove *35*

T
Tambora, Mount 28
temples 47, *53*, *55*, *100*, 102–3, *102*, *103*
textiles 92, *92*
Timor 30, 118
Tjokroaminto, Omar Said 69
Toba, Lake 23
tourism 96–7, *97*
trade 51, 55–6, *57–8*, *84*, 91, *91*
transportation 93–6, *93*
Tribhuvana 54
Trowulan 54–5

U
Ujung Kulon National Park 16, 20, 39

V
volcanoes 13, 16, *17*, 18–19, *18*, *19*, 20, 28, *29*

W
Wahid, Abdurrahman 79
Wallacea 38, 40, 42
Wallace line 42
Wasur National Park 40
wildlife 13, *36*, *37–40*
wood 85
workforce *83*, 90
World War Two 71

Y
Yogyakarta 46–7, *46* (map), *47*

Acknowledgements

Cover photo credit
Corbis: Dennis Degnan

Photo credits:
AnthroArcheArt.org: Philip Baird 53, 55, 102, 103; **Corbis:** Bettmann 50, Bojan Brecelj 35, Jack Fields 112, Wolfgang Kaehler 21, 32, Cho Sung-Su 116, Santana Wally 79, Michael S. Yamashita 27; **Ecoscene:** Colin Conway 106, Michael Maconachie 41; **Hemera Photo-Objects:** 8; **Hutchison Picture Library:** 6, Adrian Arbib 38, Jackum Brown 43, Juliet Highet 92, Jeremy Horner 29, Macintyre 12; **Mary Evans Picture Library:** 19, 48, 57, 61, 65, 66; **NHPA:** Daniel Heuclin 25; **Photodisc, Inc:** Glen Allison 26; **Rex Features:** SIPA 95; **Robert Hunt Library:** 71, 73, 75, 77, 90; **Skyscan:** Jez O'Hare 33, 45, 96, 104; **Still Pictures:** Alain Compost 36, Jean-Leo Dugast 82, Mark Edwards 86, Paul Harrison 108, 110, Gerard & Margi Moss 18, Dario Novellino 87, Hartmut Schwarzbach 56, Roland Seitre 31; **Sylvia Cordaiy Photo Library:** Chris McCall 84, Stephen Coyne 100; **Topham Picturepoint:** 68, Edy Purnomo/The Image Works 98, 119, The British Library/HIP 58, 60; **Travel Ink:** Abbie Enock 97, Patrick Ford 88, Nigel McCarthy 94; **www.planetware.com:** Jim Steinhart 47.